The
TOPICAL
HANDBOOK
of BIBLE
PROPHECY

RON
RHODES

HARVEST HOUSE PUBLISHERS

EUGENE, OREGON

Cover by Dugan Design Group, Bloomington, Minnesota

Cover photo © dundanim #10470358 / fotolia

THE TOPICAL HANDBOOK OF BIBLE PROPHECY
Copyright © 2010 by Ron Rhodes
Published by Harvest House Publishers
Eugene, Oregon 97402
www.harvesthousepublishers.com

Library of Congress Cataloging-in-Publication Data
Rhodes, Ron.
The topical handbook of Bible prophecy / Ron Rhodes.
    p. cm.
ISBN 978-0-7369-2847-2 (pbk.)
1. Bible—Prophecies. 2. End of the world—Biblical teaching. 3. Eschatology—Biblical
teaching. I. Title.
BS647.3.R45 2010
236'.903—dc22

2009047457

Printed in the United States of America

10 11 12 13 14 15 16 17 18 / BP-SK / 10 9 8 7 6 5 4 3 2 1

To my beloved Kerri

Acknowledgments

Writing this book has been a labor of love. The work process was made all the more enjoyable by the unending support of my dear wife, Kerri, and my two college-age children, David and Kylie. I never tire of thanking them.

A special thanks also goes to Bob Hawkins, Jr., and his fine, friendly team at Harvest House Publishers for getting behind the project.

Introduction

The study of end-times prophecy is known in theological circles as eschatology. This term is derived from two Greek words: *eschatos* (last things) and *logos* (study of). Eschatology is the study of last things, or of the end times.

Eschatology includes two primary fields of study. *Personal eschatology* concerns such things as salvation, death, the intermediate state, heaven, and hell. These matters are related to individuals. *General eschatology* concerns more general matters, such as the rapture, the tribulation, the second coming of Christ, the millennial kingdom, judgment, and the eternal state. This topical guide contains Bible references to common terms related to both personal and general eschatology.

You will also find references in this topical guide to what might be considered secondary terms, but these terms are quite relevant to biblical prophecy. For example, the guide includes the best biblical references on these topics:

- *Foreknowledge and omniscience.* God declares the end from the beginning.

- *The inspiration and inerrancy of Scripture.* This provides the reason we can trust biblical prophecy.

- *Interpretation of Scripture.* Without a literal interpretation, prophecy would not make sense.

- *Worry and anxiety.* Some biblical prophecies can be a bit frightening, but they are intended to encourage.

Inclusion of such terms makes this *Topical Handbook of Bible Prophecy* all the more beneficial for Bible study.

This guide has been designed to help you find Bible verses on prophetic topics quickly and easily. The topics are arranged alphabetically so you can speedily flip to your topic of interest.

May the Lord bless you as you study His Word!

The Topical Handbook
of Bible Prophecy

666

The number of the beast and of man—*Revelation 13:18*

144,000

12,000 from the tribe of Asher—*Revelation 7:6*
12,000 from the tribe of Benjamin—*Revelation 7:8*
12,000 from the tribe of Gad—*Revelation 7:5*
12,000 from the tribe of Issachar—*Revelation 7:7*
12,000 from the tribe of Joseph—*Revelation 7:8*
12,000 from the tribe of Judah—*Revelation 7:5*
12,000 from the tribe of Levi—*Revelation 7:7*
12,000 from the tribe of Manasseh—*Revelation 7:6*
12,000 from the tribe of Naphtali—*Revelation 7:6*
12,000 from the tribe of Reuben—*Revelation 7:5*
12,000 from the tribe of Simeon—*Revelation 7:7*
12,000 from the tribe of Zebulun—*Revelation 7:8*
Honest and blameless—*Revelation 14:5*
Lamb and Father's name on their foreheads—*Revelation 14:1*
Learn a new song—*Revelation 14:3*
Not defiled with women—*Revelation 14:4*
Redeemed—*Revelation 14:3*
Sealed from every tribe—*Revelation 7:4*
See Jews

200 MILLION

Led by four fallen angels—*Revelation 9:14-15*
Demonic spirits that murder millions of people—*Revelation 9:16-19*

ABADDON

The destroyer angel who reigns over the abyss—*Revelation 9:11*
Called *Apollyon* in Greek—*Revelation 9:11*
See Devil; Demons; Satan

ABOMINATION OF DESOLATION

Antichrist puts his image in the Jewish temple—*Daniel 9:27; 11:31; see also 12:11*
Antichrist reflects Satan's desire for godhood—*Isaiah 14:13-14; Ezekiel 28:2-9*
Jews to flee to the mountains—*Matthew 24:15-16*
See Antichrist

ABRAHAMIC COVENANT

Continues forever—*Psalm 105:5-11*
Includes many blessings—*Genesis 12:1-3; 15:18-21*
Reaffirmed with Isaac—*Genesis 17:21*
Reaffirmed with Jacob—*Genesis 35:10-12*
See Joshua 1:2-6; 21:43-45; 1 Chronicles 16:15-18; Isaiah 49:6; Jeremiah 25:9-12; Ezekiel 37:21-25; Daniel 9:2; Amos 9:14-15; Acts 1:6-7; 3:19-21; 15:14-17; Romans 11:1-32; Hebrews 11:8-10,12-16; Revelation 7:4
See Covenants, Biblical

ABRAHAM'S BOSOM

Abraham is in the kingdom of heaven—*Matthew 8:11*
Separation between the saved and unsaved—*Luke 16:26*
Metaphorical description of heaven—*Luke 16:23*
See Heaven; Intermediate State

ABYSS

Abode of imprisoned demons (disobedient spirits)—*Revelation 9:1-14*

Bottomless pit—*Revelation 9:1-2,11; 11:7; 17:8; 20:1,3*

The deep—*Luke 8:31; Romans 10:7*

Demons dread to go there—*Luke 8:31*

Satan is bound there during the millennial kingdom—*Revelation 20:1-3*

Smoke ascends from there—*Revelation 9:1*

See Devil; Demons

AGES OF TIME

A day is like a thousand years to the Lord—*2 Peter 3:8*

God set the boundaries for day and night—*Job 26:10*

In the beginning God created—*Genesis 1:1*

Jesus is the Creator of the universe (literally, the ages)—*Hebrews 1:2*

Signs mark off the seasons—*Genesis 1:14*

The universe (literally, the ages) was formed at God's command—*Hebrews 11:3*

See Eternity

ALPHA AND OMEGA

Jesus—*Revelation 22:12-13*

Yahweh—*Isaiah 44:6; 48:12*

See Jesus Christ, *Names and Titles*

AMERICA IN BIBLICAL PROPHECY

(Speculative suggestions)

Babylon?—*Revelation 17–18*

Land divided by rivers?—*Isaiah 18:1-7*

Land of Tarshish?—*Ezekiel 38:13*

One of the nations?—*Isaiah 66:18-20; Haggai 2:6-7; Zechariah 12:2-3*

Amos

Prophet to northern kingdom of Israel—*Amos 7:14-15*
Focused on social injustice—*Amos 5:24*
Prophesied the day of judgment—*Amos 7:1–9:10*

Ancient of Days

Yahweh—*Daniel 7:9,13,22*
Angels serve Him—*Daniel 7:10*
Clothing white as snow, hair like wool, fiery throne—*Daniel 7:9*
Jesus described in similar terms—*Revelation 1:14-16*

Angels

100 million—*Daniel 7:10*
Believers will judge angels—*1 Corinthians 6:3*
Cherubim guard the tree of life—*Genesis 3:24*
Created at God's command—*Psalm 148:2,5*
Created before the earth—*Job 38:7*
Elect—*1 Timothy 5:21*
Involved in earthly affairs—*Matthew 24:36; Luke 15:7,10;
    1 Timothy 5:21; 1 Peter 1:12*
Innumerable—*Hebrews 12:22*
Not to be worshipped—*Colossians 2:18; Revelation 19:9-10; 22:8-9*
Man is a little lower than angels—*Psalm 8:5*
Michael is the archangel—*Jude 9*
Seraphim proclaim God's holiness—*Isaiah 6:1-3*
War in heaven—*Revelation 12:7*
Will not rule the world—*Hebrews 2:5*
See Demons; Satan

Activities Among Believers

Bring messages—*Acts 10:3-33*
Escort believers to heaven—*Luke 16:22*
Give encouragement—*Acts 27:23-24*
Give guidance—*Acts 8:26*

Guard and protect—*Psalm 91:11; Matthew 18:10*

Medium of revelation to prophets—*2 Kings 1:15; Daniel 4:13-17; 8:19; 9:21-27; 10:10-20; Zechariah 1:9-11; Acts 8:26; Galatians 3:19; Hebrews 2:2; Revelation 1:1; 5:2-14; 7:1-3,11-17; 8:2-13; 22:6,16*

Protected Elisha—*2 Kings 6:15-17*

Shut the mouths of lions—*Daniel 6:22*

Used by God to answer prayer—*Acts 12:5,7-10*

Activities Among Unbelievers

Angel of death—*2 Samuel 24:16*

Announce judgments—*Revelation 14:6-10*

Execute judgments—*Genesis 19:1,13; 2 Samuel 24:16-17; 2 Kings 19:35; 1 Chronicles 21:15-16; 2 Chronicles 32:21; Psalms 35:5-6; 78:49; Isaiah 37:36; Matthew 13:41-42; Acts 12:23; 27:23-24; Jude 14–15; Revelation 7:1-2; 9:15; 15:1*

Promote evangelism—*Acts 8:26-39*

Rejoice when sinners repent—*Luke 15:7*

Restrain wickedness—*Genesis 19:10-13*

Activities in the End Times

Give instructions—*Revelation 7:2-3; 14:15*

Make proclamations—*Revelation 5:2; 14:6,8-10*

Involved with Jesus

Announced His birth—*Luke 2:9-11*

Bow before Him in heaven—*1 Peter 3:22*

Christ created angels—*Colossians 1:16*

Christ is above all angels—*Ephesians 1:20-21; Hebrews 1:4*

Strengthened Jesus after temptations—*Matthew 4:11*

Strengthened Jesus in Gethsemane—*Luke 22:43*

Will accompany Christ at second coming—*Matthew 25:31; Mark 8:38; 2 Thessalonians 1:7; Jude 14-15*

With Christ at future judgment—*Matthew 13:39-49; 16:27; 24:31; 25:31; Mark 13:27*

Nature of
> Can appear as humans—*Hebrews 13:2*
> Distinct from humans—*Psalm 8:4-5*
> Do not marry—*Matthew 22:30*
> Have emotions—*Luke 2:13*
> Have intellects—*1 Peter 1:12*
> Have wills—*Jude 6*
> Invisible—*2 Kings 6:17*
> Ministering spirits—*Hebrews 1:14*
> Powerful—*Psalm 103:20*

Ranks of Angels
> Archangel—*Jude 9*
> Cherubim—*Genesis 3:22-24*
> Chief princes—*Daniel 10:13*
> Different ranks—*Ephesians 3:10; Colossians 1:16*
> Guardian angels—*Matthew 18:10*
> Ruling angels—*Ephesians 3:10*
> Seraphim—*Isaiah 6:1-3*

ANIMAL SACRIFICES IN THE MILLENNIAL TEMPLE
See Millennial Kingdom; Sacrifices, Millennial; Temple

ANNIHILATIONISM*
Hell includes degrees of punishment—*Matthew 10:15; 11:21-24; 16:27; Luke 12:47-48; Hebrews 10:29; Revelation 20:11-15; 22:12*

The punishment of the wicked is eternal—*Matthew 25:46*
See Hell

ANTICHRIST
The beast—*Revelation 13:1-10*

---

* Annihilationism is the unbiblical view that the unsaved do not suffer in hell but rather cease to exist.

Commercial genius—*Daniel 11:43; Revelation 13:16-17*
Destiny is lake of fire—*Revelation 19:20*
Reigns during the tribulation—*Revelation 13*
Emerges from the reunited Roman empire—*Daniel 7:8; 9:26*
Energized by Satan—*2 Thessalonians 2:9*
The false prophet will seek to make world worship him—
  Revelation 13:11-12
Headquartered in Rome—*Revelation 17:8-9*
Will revive Roman empire—*Daniel 2; 7*
People will worship him—*Revelation 13:8*
An intellectual genius—*Daniel 8:23*
Is coming—*1 John 2:18*
Is now restrained—*2 Thessalonians 2:6*
Makes a covenant with Israel—*Daniel 9:27*
The man of lawlessness—*2 Thessalonians 2:1-10*
A military genius—*Revelation 6:2; 13:2*
A political genius—*Revelation 17:11-12*
Rises out of the sea (Gentile nations)—*Revelation 13:1; 17:15*
Sets up his own kingdom—*Revelation 13*
Son of perdition—*2 Thessalonians 2:3*
Speaks arrogant, boastful words—*2 Thessalonians 2:4*
Spirit of Antichrist—*1 John 4:3*
Defeated by Jesus at second coming—*2 Thessalonians 2:8;
  Revelation 19:11-16*
Deceives many—*Revelation 19:20*
Rules whole world—*Revelation 13:3,7*
Persecutes Christians—*Revelation 13:7*
Works counterfeit signs and wonders—*2 Thessalonians 2:9-10*
See Beasts; Satan; Tribulation Period

Spirit of Antichrist
Deceives—*2 John 7*
Denies Christ came in flesh—*1 John 4:2-3*

Denies Father and Son—*1 John 2:22*
In the world already—*1 John 4:3*
Prevalent in apostolic times—*1 John 2:18*
Related to false prophets—*1 John 4:1*

Descriptions of Antichrist
The beast—*Revelation 11:7; see also 13:1; 14:9; 15:2; 16:2; 17:3,13;
19:20; 20:10*
A despicable person—*Daniel 11:21*
The lawless one—*2 Thessalonians 2:8*
The little horn—*Daniel 7:8*
The man of lawlessness—*2 Thessalonians 2:3*
The one who makes desolate—*Daniel 9:27*
The prince who is to come—*Daniel 9:26*
The son of destruction—*2 Thessalonians 2:3*

Anti-Semitism

Jews ordered out of Rome—*Acts 18:1-2*
Jews persecuted—*Nehemiah 1:1-3*
Jews persecuted in end times—*Revelation 12:5-6*
A plot to destroy Jews—*Esther 3:1-6*
See Tribulation Martyrdom

Apocalypse

Book of Revelation (Greek, *apokalupsis*)—*Revelation 1:1*
See Revelation, Book of

Apocalyptic Literature

See Seventy Weeks of Daniel; Revelation, Book of

Apostasy

Warnings against—*Hebrews 6:5-8; 10:26*
Demas—*2 Timothy 4:10*
Hymenaeus and Alexander—*1 Timothy 1:19-20*

Judas—*Matthew 26:14-25,47-57; 27:3-10*

End-times apostasy—*2 Thessalonians 2:3; see also Matthew 24:10-12*

Encouraged by false teachers—*Matthew 24:11; Galatians 2:4*

Departure from faith, doctrines of demons—*1 Timothy 4:1-2*

Sound teaching ignored—*2 Timothy 4:3-4*

During trials—*Matthew 24:9-10; Luke 8:13*

ARCHANGEL

At the rapture—*1 Thessalonians 4:16*

Michael and the devil—*Jude 1:9*

See Angels

ARK OF THE COVENANT

Contained Aaron's rod—*Numbers 17:10*

Contained a pot of manna—*Exodus 16:33*

Contained the tablets of the law—*Exodus 25:16,21*

Not missed or replaced—*Jeremiah 3:16*

Blood sprinkled upon—*Leviticus 23:27*

Kept in Holy of Holies—*Exodus 26:33*

May resurface for Jewish tribulation temple—*Daniel 9:24-27; Matthew 24:15; 2 Thessalonians 2:4; Revelation 11:1-2*

Symbolized God's presence—*1 Samuel 4:3-22*

ARMAGEDDON

Armageddon means "Mount of Megiddo"—*Revelation 16:16*

Prior to second coming—*Revelation 16:16*

Catastrophic series of battles—*Daniel 11:40-45; Joel 3:9-17; Zechariah 14:1-3; Revelation 16:14-16*

Devastating to humanity—*Matthew 24:22*

The final battle—*Revelation 16:14,16*

Antichrist's allies are assembled—*Psalm 2:1-6; Joel 3:9-11; Revelation 16:12-16*

Antichrist's armies at Bozrah—*Jeremiah 49:13-14*

Battle from Bozrah to Valley of Jehoshaphat—*Jeremiah 49:20-22; Joel 3:12-13; Zechariah 14:12-15*

Antichrist's campaign into Egypt—*Daniel 11:40-45*

Babylon destroyed—*Isaiah 13–14; Jeremiah 50–51; Zechariah 5:5-11; Revelation 17–18*

Christ on the Mount of Olives—*Joel 3:14-17; Zechariah 14:3-5; Matthew 24:29-31; Revelation 16:17-21; 19:11-21*

Jerusalem falls—*Micah 4:11–5:1; Zechariah 12–14*

Siege of Jerusalem—*Zechariah 14:2*

War on the great day of God—*Revelation 16:14*

Israel regenerated—*Psalm 79:1-13; Isaiah 64:1-12; Hosea 6:1-11; Joel 2:28-32; Zechariah 12:10; Romans 11:25-27*

Climaxes with Christ's return—*Isaiah 34:1-7; Micah 2:12-13; Habakkuk 3:3; Revelation 19:11-21*

No one would survive if not for Christ's coming—*Matthew 24:22*

See Second Coming of Christ; Tribulation Period

ASTROLOGY

Astrologers denounced by God—*Isaiah 47:15*

Astrologers lack discernment—*Daniel 2:2,10*

Condemned as occultism—*Deuteronomy 18:9-12; 2 Kings 17:16; Jeremiah 10:2; Acts 7:42*

Worshipping heavenly bodies forbidden—*Deuteronomy 4:19*

See Occultism

ASTRONOMICAL SIGNS (COSMIC DISTURBANCES)

In the tribulation—*Revelation 6:12; 8:5,12*

At the second coming—*Matthew 24:29-30*

See Isaiah 13:10; 24:23; Ezekiel 32:7; Joel 2:10,31; 3:15; Amos 5:20; 8:9; Zephaniah 1:15; Acts 2:20; Hebrews 12:26

B

BABYLON
Opposed to God and His people—*2 Kings 24:10; Lamentations 1:1-7*
Center of false religion—*Revelation 17:4-5; 18:1-2*
Center of world commerce—*Revelation 18:9-19*
Global importance—*Revelation 17:15,18*
Shinar—*Genesis 10:10*
Literal city in end times—*Revelation 17:18*
Persecutes God's people—*Revelation 17:6; 18:20,24*
Revived by Antichrist—*Revelation 18*

BALAAM
Led Israelites away from Lord—*Numbers 22–24*
Teaching deceived believers in Pergamum—*Revelation 2:14*

BEASTS
Antichrist (first beast)—*Revelation 13:1-3*
Antichrist empowered by Satan—*Revelation 13:2*
False prophet (second beast)—*Revelation 13:11*
The second beast promotes worship of the first beast—*Revelation 13:13-15*
Thrown in the lake of fire—*Revelation 19:20*
See Antichrist; False Prophet

BEATIFIC VISION IN HEAVEN
We will see God face-to-face—*Revelation 22:4; see also 1 Corinthians 13:12*
We will see God's likeness—*Psalm 17:15*
We shall see Him as He is—*1 John 3:2*
See Heaven

BEMA
See Judgment Seat of Christ

BETH-TOGARMAH (MODERN TURKEY)

Member of coalition that will invade Israel—*Ezekiel 38:1-6; see also 27:14*

From the north—*Ezekiel 38:6*

See Ezekiel Invasion; Northern Coalition

BIBLE

All-sufficient—*Deuteronomy 8:3; 30:14; Luke 16:29-31*

Enduring—*Psalms 93:5; 119:89,91; Matthew 5:17-18; Luke 16:16-17; 21:33; John 10:35; 1 Peter 1:23*

Eternal—*Psalms 19:9; 119:89,152,160; Isaiah 40:6-8; Matthew 24:35*

Illuminating—*Psalm 119:105,130,133; 2 Peter 1:19; 1 John 2:8*

Inspired—*2 Samuel 23:1-2; Nehemiah 9:13-14; Acts 1:15-16; Romans 1:2; 1 Corinthians 14:36-37; Galatians 1:11-12; 1 Thessalonians 2:13; 2 Timothy 3:16; 1 Peter 1:10-12; 2 Peter 1:20-21; 1 John 5:9*

Instructive—*Psalm 119:24,169; Romans 15:4; 2 Timothy 3:14-17*

Record of revelation—*Exodus 17:14; 24:4; Joshua 8:32; 24:26; 2 Chronicles 26:22; Jeremiah 30:2; 45:1-2; Habakkuk 2:2; John 20:30-31; Revelation 1:10-11,17-19; 22:18-19*

Reliable—*1 Kings 8:56; Psalms 19:9; 105:19; 111:5; 119:140; Proverbs 22:19-21; Ezekiel 12:25; Luke 24:44*

Right—*Psalms 19:8; 33:4; 119:128,137,144*

A safeguard—*Psalms 17:4-5; 19:9,11; 119:9,11,25,116*

Standard of truth—*Matthew 15:1-3; Mark 7:7-9,13; John 5:46-47; Acts 18:28; 28:23*

Sure—*Psalm 19:9*

True—*1 Kings 17:24; Psalms 33:4; 119:43,142,151,160; Proverbs 22:20-21; Ecclesiastes 12:10; Daniel 10:21; John 17:17; 21:24; Ephesians 1:13; Colossians 1:3-6; 2 Timothy 2:15; James 1:18; Revelation 19:9; 21:5*

Trustworthy—*2 Samuel 7:28; Psalms 19:7; 111:7; 119:42,86,138; Revelation 22:6*

BINDING OF SATAN

In bottomless pit during millennial kingdom—*Revelation 20:1-3*

Pit is place of imprisonment for demons—*Luke 8:31; 2 Peter 2:4*

Loosed at end of millennial kingdom to deceive nations—*Revelation 20:7-9*

Judged and cast into lake of fire—*Matthew 25:46; Revelation 20:10*

See Devil; Satan; Demons

BIRTH PANGS, TRIBULATION

Beginning of birth pains—*Matthew 24:8*

Includes false Christs, wars, famines, and earthquakes—*Matthew 24:4-7*

See Tribulation Period

BLASPHEMY

Antichrist's names and words—*Revelation 13:5-6; 17:3*

Antichrist's nature—*2 Thessalonians 2:3-11*

Claiming divinity for oneself—*Mark 14:64; John 10:33*

Denying the true identity of Jesus as Messiah—*Luke 22:65; John 10:36*

Lack of reverence or contempt for God—*Leviticus 24:16; Matthew 26:65; Mark 2:7*

Speaking evil against God—*Psalm 74:18; Isaiah 52:5; Romans 2:24; Revelation 13:1,6; 16:9,11,21*

BLESSED HOPE, RAPTURE

Rapture of church—*Titus 2:13; see also Romans 8:22-23; 1 Corinthians 15:51-58; Philippians 3:20-21; 1 Thessalonians 4:13-18; 1 John 3:2-3*

See Rapture

BLINDNESS, ISRAEL'S

Stumbled over "stumbling stone," Jesus Christ—*Romans 9:31-33*

Refused to believe in Christ—*Matthew 12:14,24*

Hardened—*Romans 11:25*

Jealous of Gentiles—*Romans 11:11*

Remnant saved—*Romans 11:25*

End-times repentance—*Isaiah 53:1-9; Zechariah 12:10; Matthew 23:37-39*

See Israel, *Rebirth of*

Book of Life

Alternative is the lake of fire—*Revelation 20:15*

Book of the living—*Psalm 69:28*

The church of the firstborn—*Hebrews 12:23*

Records the names of the redeemed—*Revelation 3:5; 13:8; 17:8; 20:12,15; 21:27*

Moses referred to God's book—*Exodus 32:32-33*

Names of believers in the book—*Philippians 4:3*

Names of believers not blotted out—*Revelation 3:5*

Names of God's elect inscribed from the foundation of the world—*Revelation 17:8*

Rejoice—*Luke 10:20*

Bottomless Pit

See Abyss

Bowl Judgments

Seven bowls—*Revelation 16:2-21*

Catastrophic Events

Activity of unclean spirits—*Revelation 16:13*

A devastating earthquake—*Revelation 16:18*

Darkness—*Revelation 16:10*

Destruction—*Revelation 16:19*

People receive painful sores—*Revelation 16:2*

People scorched by sun—*Revelation 16:8-9*

Rivers dry up—*Revelation 16:12*
Sea creatures die—*Revelation 16:3-4*
Water turns to blood—*Revelation 16:3-4*

BRIDEGROOM AND HIS BRIDE

The church awaits her Bridegroom—*2 Corinthians 11:2; Revelation 19:7-9*
Jesus prepares His home for His bride—*John 14:1-3*
The marriage and marriage supper of the Lamb—*Revelation 19:7-10*
The parable of ten virgins—*Matthew 25:1-13*
See Church

Church

A "new man"—*Ephesians 2:15*
Equality in the church—*Galatians 3:26-28*
The body of Christ—*Colossians 1:18*
The bride of Christ—*Revelation 21:2*
Will reign with Christ—*Revelation 20:4,6*
God's temple—*1 Corinthians 3:16*
Jesus builds it—*Matthew 16:18*
Jesus purchased it—*Acts 20:28*
God's household—*Ephesians 2:19-20; 1 Timothy 3:14-15*
One body with many members—*Romans 12:4-5; 1 Corinthians 12:12*
A spiritual house—*1 Peter 2:4-5*

Christ's Authority

Christ is the cornerstone—*Ephesians 2:20; 1 Peter 2:7*
Christ is in authority—*Ephesians 1:22; Colossians 2:10*
Christ is the foundation—*1 Corinthians 3:11*
Christ is the head—*Ephesians 4:15; 5:23; Colossians 1:18; 2:19*

Discipline

Restoration after—*2 Corinthians 2:6-8*
Correction—*Titus 2:15*
Discipline—*2 Corinthians 2:6-11*
Disobedience calls for—*2 Thessalonians 3:14*
Commendation for—*Revelation 2:2*
Church in Pergamum rebuked by Jesus—*Revelation 2:14-16*
Protocol for discipline—*Matthew 18:15-17*
Rebuke when necessary—*Titus 1:13*
Restore with gentleness—*Galatians 6:1*
Restore and save those who wander—*James 5:19-20*
For sexual immorality—*1 Corinthians 5:1-11*

Distinct from Israel

The church began on the Day of Pentecost, not in Old Testament—*Acts 1:5; 1 Corinthians 12:13*

The church is future from time of Jesus—*Matthew 16:18; Ephesians 3:1-10*

Israel is composed of Jews; the church includes Jews and Gentiles—*1 Corinthians 10:32; Ephesians 2:15*

Israel is a political entity; the church is the spiritual body of Christ—*Exodus 19:5-6; Ephesians 1:3*

Israel will be restored before Christ returns—*Romans 11:1-2,26-29*

Promises to Israel will be fulfilled—*Genesis 13:1-7; 2 Samuel 7:12-16*

Government

Deacons—*Acts 6:1-6*

Elders—*Acts 14:23; Titus 1:5*

Instructions to elders—*Acts 20:17,28; 1 Peter 5:1-4*

Qualifications for elders and deacons—*1 Timothy 3:1-13; Titus 1:6-9*

Growth

Many Gentiles believed—*Acts 11:20-21*

Many believed in Lord—*Acts 9:42*

Many were brought to Lord—*Acts 5:14*

One body, many members—*1 Corinthians 12:12; Ephesians 5:29-30*

Those who believed were added—*Acts 2:41,47*

Mission

Christ's witnesses—*Luke 24:45-49; Acts 1:7-8*

Build up body of Christ—*Ephesians 4:11-13*

Do good to all people—*Galatians 6:10; Titus 3:14*

Exercise spiritual gifts—*Romans 12:6-8*

Financially support God's work—*1 Corinthians 16:1-3*
Help brothers in need—*1 John 3:16-18*
Love each other—*Hebrews 13:1-3,16*
Make disciples—*Matthew 28:19-20*
Offer hospitality to each other—*1 Peter 4:9-11*
Preach the Word—*Mark 16:15-16; 1 Timothy 4:6,13*
Take care of orphans and widows—*1 Timothy 5:3-4,16; James 1:27*
Care for the sick—*James 5:14-15*

Prophecy and the Church

Apostasy in the end times—*2 Thessalonians 2:3; 1 Timothy 4:1-5; 2 Timothy 3:1-5*
Heresy in the last days—*2 Timothy 4:3*
Raptured before the tribulation—*1 Thessalonians 4:13-17*
In heaven during the tribulation—*Revelation 4–18*
The bride of Christ—*Revelation 19:7*
Reigns with Christ—*2 Timothy 2:12; Revelation 20:6*
Will live in the New Jerusalem—*John 14:1-3; Revelation 21*

Unity

Jesus' prayer—*John 17:21*
One body—*1 Corinthians 10:17; 12:12; Ephesians 4:4,12,13,16,25*
One flock, one shepherd—*John 10:16*
Peace between Jews and Gentiles—*Ephesians 2:14,21*
United—*John 17:11*

CHURCH AGE

Yet future from Jesus' perspective—*Matthew 16:18*
Inaugurated after Jesus' resurrection—*Ephesians 1:20-22*
Inaugurated after Jesus' ascension—*Ephesians 4:7-12*
Began at the Day of Pentecost—*Acts 2; 11:15-16*

Closes at the rapture—*1 Corinthians 15:50-58; 1 Thessalonians 4:13-17*

The church is a mystery—*Ephesians 3:3-5,9; Colossians 1:26-27*

CITY OF GOD

Builder is Christ—*John 14:1-3*

Builder is God—*Hebrews 11:10*

The holy habitation of the Most High—*Psalm 46:4*

New Jerusalem, the heavenly city—*Revelation 3:12*

See Heaven

CONVERSION OF ISRAEL

Israel is now blind—*Romans 9:32*

Gospel is now preached to Gentiles, causing Jewish jealousy—*Romans 11:11*

Israel will repent and turn to the Messiah—*Isaiah 53:1-9; Zechariah 12:10; Matthew 23:37-39*

See Israel, *Rebirth of*

COSMIC DISTURBANCES

See Astronomical Signs

COVENANT, ANTICHRIST AND ISRAEL

Antichrist signs seven-year covenant—*Daniel 9:24-27*

Israel's security and rest a precondition for Ezekiel invasion—*Ezekiel 38:1-6,18*

COVENANTS, BIBLICAL

Noahic covenant—*Genesis 6:18; 9:8-17*

Abrahamic covenant—*Genesis 12:1-3*

Davidic covenant—*2 Samuel 7:5-17*

Mosaic covenant—*Exodus 19:3-6; 20–40*

New covenant—*Jeremiah 31:31-34*

Palestinian covenant—*Deuteronomy 30*

Gentiles partake of the spiritual blessings of Jewish covenants—
Romans 11:17; 15:25-27; Ephesians 2:11-16; 3:5-6
See Abrahamic Covenant; Davidic Covenant; New Covenant

CREATION AND HEAVEN

CREATION	HEAVEN
division of light and darkness (Genesis 1:4)	no night (Revelation 21:25)
division of land and sea (Genesis 1:10)	no more sea (Revelation 21:1)
rule of sun and moon (Genesis 1:16)	no need of sun or moon (Revelation 21:23)
man in prepared garden (Genesis 2:8-9)	man in prepared city (Revelation 21:2)
river flowing from Eden (Genesis 2:10)	river flowing from God's throne (Revelation 22:1)
tree of life in garden (Genesis 2:9)	tree of life throughout city (Revelation 22:2)
man in God's image (Genesis 1:27)	man in God's presence (Revelation 21:3)
Satan opposes (Genesis 3:15)	Satan vanquished (Revelation 20:10)
Redeemer promised (Genesis 3:15)	redemption accomplished (Revelation 5:9-10)
cursed ground (Genesis 3:17)	no more curse (Revelation 22:3)
daily sorrow (Genesis 3:17)	no more sorrow (Revelation 21:4)
return to dust (Genesis 3:19)	no more death (Revelation 21:4)
kept from tree of life (Genesis 3:24)	access to tree of life (Revelation 22:14)
cherubim guarding (Genesis 3:24)	angels inviting (Revelation 21:9)

CROWNS AND FUTURE REWARDS

All believers will be judged—*Romans 14:8-10*

Believers lay their crowns before the throne—*Revelation 4:10*

Incorruptible—*1 Corinthians 9:25*

Crown of glory—*1 Peter 5:4*

Crown of life—*James 1:12; Revelation 2:10*

Crown of righteousness—*2 Timothy 4:8*

Some believers will be ashamed at Christ's coming—*1 John 2:28*

Some believers may lose rewards—*2 John 8*

See Judgment Seat of Christ

CUSH (MODERN SUDAN)

In coalition that will invade Israel—*Ezekiel 38:5; see also Genesis 2:13; 10:6-8; 2 Kings 19:9; 1 Chronicles 1:8-10; Psalms 68:31; 87:4; Isaiah 11:11; 18:1; 20:3,5; 37:9; 43:3; 45:14; Jeremiah 46:9; Ezekiel 29:10; 30:4-5,9; Nahum 3:9; Zephaniah 3:10*

See Ezekiel Invasion; Northern Coalition

DATE OF THE RAPTURE

Always be ready—*Matthew 25:1-13*

Be sober and alert until Christ comes—*Mark 13:32-37*

Timing is in God's hands—*Acts 1:7*

DAVIDIC COVENANT

David's descendant will rule forever—*2 Samuel 7:12-13; 22:51; 1 Chronicles 17:10-14*

Fulfilled in Jesus—*Matthew 1:1; Luke 1:32-33*

Jesus will rule in Jerusalem during the millennial kingdom—*Isaiah 9:6-7; Jeremiah 23:5-6; 33:17-26; Ezekiel 36:1-12; Amos 9:11-12; Micah 4:1-5; Zephaniah 3:14-20; Zechariah 14:1-21*

See Covenants, Biblical

DAY OF THE LORD

Judgment in tribulation—*2 Thessalonians 2:2; Revelation 16–18*

Judgment on Israel for disobedience—*Isaiah 3:18–4:1; Amos 5:18-20*

Judgment on nations that oppress Israel—*Isaiah 13:1-22; Obadiah 15*

Judgment that will usher in new earth—*2 Peter 3:10-13; Revelation 20:7–21:1*

Deliverance and blessing for Israel—*Isaiah 11:10-12; Joel 3:14-18*

And the second coming—*1 Corinthians 5:5; 1 Thessalonians 5:2; 2 Thessalonians 2:2; 2 Peter 3:10,12*

Will come like thief in night—*1 Thessalonians 5:2*

Heavens will be destroyed—*2 Peter 3:10; see also Isaiah 65:17-19; 66:22; Revelation 21:1*

See Tribulation Period

DEATH

All people die—*Job 30:23; Ecclesiastes 7:1-2; 8:8*

Followed by resurrection for all—*Acts 24:15*

Followed by judgment—*Hebrews 9:27*

Ananias and Sapphira—*Acts 5:1-10*

Jesus was aware of His imminent death—*John 18:4*

A body without a spirit is dead—*James 2:26*

Judgment for Israel's unwillingness to go into the promised land—*Numbers 14:29,32-33*

Swallowed up by God—*Isaiah 25:8*

Conquered by Christ—*Romans 6:9; 1 Corinthians 15:54-56; 2 Timothy 1:10; Hebrews 2:15; Revelation 1:18*

Corpses—*1 Kings 13:24; 2 Kings 19:35; Nahum 3:3*

Creator's power over—*Mark 5:38-42*

Death preferred—*Numbers 20:3; 1 Kings 19:4*

Death promised for disobedience—*Genesis 2:16-17*

Death results from sin—*Romans 5:12*

Death's terrors—*Psalm 55:4*

Departure from this life—*Genesis 23:2; 25:8; Job 1:19*

Return to this life is impossible—*Job 7:9-10; 14:10,14*

Dust to dust—*Genesis 3:19; Job 10:9*

Eagerly anticipated—*Job 3:21-22*

Earthly possessions left behind—*Job 1:21; 1 Timothy 6:7*

Earthly projects stopped—*Ecclesiastes 9:10*

Life is fleeting—*Job 14:1-2; Psalms 39:4-5; 89:47-48; 90:9; 1 Peter 1:24*

Forgotten after death—*Ecclesiastes 9:5*

God takes no pleasure in the death of wicked—*Ezekiel 18:23; 33:11*

Going down into silence—*Psalm 115:17*

Ignorance of earthly affairs—*Ecclesiastes 9:5*

Announced—*Deuteronomy 31:14*

Destroyed by Jesus—*2 Timothy 1:9-10*

Keys of death and Hades—*Revelation 1:18*

Those who believe in Jesus never die—*John 11:25-26*

Joining ancestors—*Deuteronomy 31:16*

Joy turned to sadness—*2 Samuel 19:2*
King of terrors—*Job 18:14*
Last enemy to be destroyed—*1 Corinthians 15:26*
Levels all ranks—*Job 3:17-19*
Life's final moment—*Mark 15:37-39*
Martyr's death—*Acts 7:54-56*
No one has power over the day of his death—*Ecclesiastes 8:8*
No more death—*Revelation 21:3-4*
No death in heaven—*Luke 20:36; Revelation 21:4*
Ordered by God—*Deuteronomy 32:39; Job 14:5*
Precious to the Lord—*Psalm 116:15*
Prepare—*2 Kings 20:1; Psalms 39:4; 90:12; Isaiah 38:1; Luke 12:20; 2 Timothy 4:6-8*
Return to ground—*Genesis 3:19*
Saul's disobedience—*1 Chronicles 10:13-14*
Destroyed by Christ—*Hosea 13:14; 1 Corinthians 15:26*
Sodom and Gomorrah—*Genesis 19:1-29*
Ways that lead to death—*Proverbs 14:12*
Sting of death—*1 Corinthians 15:56*
Sudden death—*Job 4:20*
Those who are no more—*Matthew 2:18*
A time to die—*Ecclesiastes 3:1-2; 7:17*
To live is Christ; to die is gain—*Philippians 1:21*
The valley of the shadow of death—*Psalm 23:4*
The wages of sin is death—*Romans 6:23*
Whether live or die, we are the Lord's—*Romans 14:8*

Consciousness After Death
Absent from body, at home with Lord—*2 Corinthians 5:8*
Rich man and Lazarus—*Luke 16:19-31*
Souls under God's altar—*Revelation 6:9*
Thief with Christ in paradise—*Luke 23:43*
See Intermediate State

Death of Christ

Appeased God's wrath—*1 John 2:2*

Brought reconciliation—*2 Corinthians 5:18-21*

Brought redemption—*Galatians 3:13*

Paid our ransom—*1 Timothy 2:6*

Death of the Righteous

In life and death, we belong to the Lord—*Romans 14:8*

Blessed are those who die in the Lord—*Revelation 14:13*

Prefer to be away from body, at home with the
Lord—*2 Corinthians 5:8*

To depart and be with Christ is better—*Philippians 1:21-23*

God will take us to Himself—*Psalm 49:15*

The righteous have a refuge when they die—*Proverbs 14:32*

The upright enter into peace and find rest—*Isaiah 57:2*

Not all of us will die—*1 Corinthians 15:51*

Precious to God—*Psalm 116:15*

Lazarus—*Luke 16:22*

Paul's anticipation—*2 Timothy 4:6-8*

Peter's anticipation—*2 Peter 1:14*

The psalmist commits his spirit to God—*Psalm 31:5*

Stephen commits his spirit to Jesus—*Acts 7:59*

Jesus commits His spirit to the Father—*Luke 23:46*

We will someday rise again—*Daniel 12:13*

We will someday receive eternal bodies—*2 Corinthians 5:1-3*

Death of the Wicked

Disaster strikes like cyclone—*Proverbs 10:25*

Egyptians killed by plague—*Psalm 78:50*

God cuts off the godless—*Job 27:8*

Ground opens and swallows Korah, Dathan, and Abiram—
Numbers 16:30

Rich man and Lazarus—*Luke 16:22*

The wicked do not anticipate death—*Luke 12:20*
The wicked are destroyed—*Psalm 37:9-10; Proverbs 2:22*
The years of the wicked are cut short—*Proverbs 10:27*

Desired

Believers—*2 Corinthians 5:2,8*
Paul—*Philippians 1:23*
Job—*Job 7:15-16; 10:1*
Jonah—*Jonah 4:3,8*
Simeon—*Luke 2:29*
The wicked (during the tribulation period)—*Revelation 9:6*

People Who Didn't (or Won't) Die

Enoch—*Genesis 5:24; Hebrews 11:5*
Elijah—*2 Kings 2:1*
Raptured Christians—*1 Corinthians 15:51; 1 Thessalonians 4:17*
See Rapture

Preparation for Death

Be mindful of the brief time on earth—*Psalm 39:4*
Be diligent—*Ecclesiastes 9:10; John 9:4*
In life and death, we belong to Lord—*Romans 14:8*
To live is Christ; to die is gain—*Philippians 1:21*
Make the most of your time on earth—*Psalm 90:12*
Set your affairs in order—*2 Kings 20:1*
Look forward to the heavenly city—*Hebrews 13:14*

Spiritual Death

Dead in sin—*Ephesians 2:1-2; Colossians 2:13*
Entered human race through Adam's sin—*Romans 5:12,15*
Banishment from God—*2 Thessalonians 1:9*
Believers will escape—*Revelation 2:11; 20:6*
Eternal darkness—*Matthew 25:30; 2 Peter 2:17*

Christ delivers from eternal death—*John 3:16; 8:51; Acts 4:12*
God can save or destroy—*Matthew 10:28; James 4:12*
Christ can save or destroy—*Matthew 25:31-41; 2 Thessalonians 1:7-8*
A consequence of sin—*Romans 6:16,21,23; 8:13; James 1:15*
The wicked deserve death—*Matthew 25:41,46; Romans 1:32*
Wages of sin—*Romans 6:23*
Second death—*Revelation 2:11; 20:6,14; 21:8*

DECEPTION IN THE END TIMES

Many will not endure sound teaching—*2 Timothy 4:3-4*
Many will succumb to doctrines of demons—*1 Timothy 4:1*
Widespread apostasy—*2 Thessalonians 2:3*
See Apostasy

DELAY OF THE SECOND COMING

God shows patience before judgment—*Joel 2:13; Luke 15:20; Romans 9:22*
God longs that all be saved, though not all will be—*1 Timothy 2:4; 2 Peter 3:9*
See Second Coming of Christ

DEMONS

Evil spirits—*Luke 7:21; 10:19-20*
Fallen angels—*Matthew 12:24-28*
Lying spirits—*1 Timothy 4:1*
Spiritual forces of wickedness—*Ephesians 6:12*
Tormenting spirit—*1 Samuel 16:14; 18:10; 19:9*
Unclean spirits—*Matthew 10:1*
Did not keep first estate—*Jude 6*
Jesus' authority over—*Matthew 4:24; 8:16*
Disciples' authority over—*Matthew 10:1*
Believers' authority over—*Mark 16:17*
Some committed unnatural sin—*Genesis 6:2-4*

Hinder answers to prayers—*Daniel 10:12-20*

Disseminate false doctrine—*1 Timothy 4:1*

Influence false prophets—*1 John 4:1-4*

Promote idolatry—*Leviticus 17:7; Deuteronomy 32:17; Psalm 106:36-38*

Torment people during the tribulation—*Revelation 9:3*

In blind and mute man—*Matthew 9:32-33; 12:22; Luke 11:14*

In land of Gadarenes—*Matthew 8:28*

In mute boy—*Mark 9:17-18*

Many can be present in one person—*Luke 8:30*

Sacrifices to—*Deuteronomy 32:17; Psalm 106:37; 1 Corinthians 10:20*

Worship of—*Revelation 9:20*

See Angels; Satan

Biblical Signs of Possible Demon Possession

(These symptoms are not always signs of demonic influence.)

Physical pain—*2 Corinthians 12:7*

Physical diseases—*Matthew 9:33; 12:22; 17:15-18*

Mental disorders—*Mark 5:4-5; 9:22; Luke 8:27-29; 9:37-42*

Self-destructive behavior—*Mark 5:5; Luke 9:42*

Jealousy and division—*James 3:13-16*

Death—*Revelation 9:14-19*

Judgment of Demons

Satan cast from original position of privilege in heaven—*Ezekiel 28:16*

Satan judged in Garden of Eden—*Genesis 3:14-15*

Satan judged at cross—*John 12:31; Colossians 2:15; Hebrews 2:14*

Satan cast from heaven in middle of tribulation—*Revelation 12:13*

Satan bound prior to millennial kingdom—*Revelation 20:10*

Satan cast into lake of fire after the millennium—*Matthew 25:41; Revelation 20:10;*

Some presently confined—*2 Peter 2:4*

Will be bound prior to millennial kingdom—*Revelation 20:10*
Destined for the lake of fire—*Matthew 25:41*

DENIAL IN END TIMES

Authority—*2 Timothy 3:4*
Christ—*1 John 2:18; 4:3*
Christ's return—*2 Peter 3:3-4*
Christian liberty—*1 Timothy 4:3-4*
The faith—*1 Timothy 4:1-2; Jude 3*
God—*Luke 17:26; 2 Timothy 3:4-5*
Morals—*2 Timothy 3:1-8,13; Jude 18*
Separated life—*2 Timothy 3:1-7*
Sound doctrine—*2 Timothy 4:3-4*
See Apostasy

DEVIL

Rebelled against God—*Isaiah 14:12-15; Ezekiel 28:13-18*
Led one-third of angels in rebellion—*Revelation 12:4*
Lied to Eve—*Genesis 3:4*
Rose up against Israel—*1 Chronicles 21:1*
Accused Job before God—*Job 1:6-9,12*
Tempted Jesus—*Matthew 4:1-11; Mark 1:13; Luke 4:2*
Worked through Peter—*Matthew 16:23*
Entered into Judas—*Luke 22:3; John 13:27*
Accuses and slanders believers—*Job 1:6-11; Revelation 12:10*
Deceives the whole world—*Revelation 12:9*
Promotes spiritual pride—*1 Timothy 3:6*
Has followers—*1 Timothy 5:15*
Hinders answers to prayers—*Daniel 10:12-20*
Promotes jealousy—*James 3:13-16*
Promotes doubt—*Genesis 3:1-5*
Possesses people—*Mark 3:22*
Masquerades as angel of light—*2 Corinthians 11:14*

Prowls like roaring lion—*1 Peter 5:8*
Tempts believers to immorality—*1 Corinthians 7:5*
Tempts believers to lie—*Acts 5:3*
Synagogue of Satan—*Revelation 2:9*
Jesus came to destroy—*Hebrews 2:14; 1 John 3:8*
Barred from heaven during the tribulation—*Revelation 12:9-10*
Will be bound for thousand years—*Revelation 20:2*
Prideful—*1 Timothy 3:6*
Resist him—*James 4:7*
Wear spiritual armor for protection—*Ephesians 6:11-18*

Names and Descriptions
The god of this world—*2 Corinthians 4:4*
A cherub—*Ezekiel 28:14*
Murderer and father of lies—*John 8:44*
Prince of demons—*Matthew 12:24*
Accuser of brethren—*Revelation 12:10*
Beelzebub—*Matthew 12:24*
Belial—*2 Corinthians 6:15*
Devil—*1 Peter 5:8*
Dragon—*Revelation 12:3*
Evil one—*1 John 5:19*
God of this age—*2 Corinthians 4:4*
Lucifer—*Isaiah 14:12*
Prince of the power of the air—*Ephesians 2:2*
Prince of this world—*John 12:31*
Satan—*2 Corinthians 11:14*
Serpent—*Revelation 12:9*
Tempter—*1 Thessalonians 3:5*
See Satan; Demons

DISPENSATIONS
Innocence—*Genesis 1:28–3:6*

Conscience—*Genesis 3:7–8:14*
Human government—*Genesis 8:15–11:9*
Promise—*Genesis 11:10–Exodus 18:27*
Israel and the law—*Exodus 19–Acts 1:26*
The church and grace—*Acts 2:1–Revelation 19:21*
The kingdom—*Revelation 20:1-16*

DIVINATION

Astrologers cannot interpret dreams—*Daniel 4:7*
Astrologers cannot save you—*Isaiah 47:13*
Consulting mediums brings judgment—*Leviticus 20:6*
Diviners will be disgraced—*Micah 3:7*
Do not call forth spirits of dead—*Deuteronomy 18:11*
Do not practice sorcery and divination—*2 Kings 21:6*
Do not listen to fortune-tellers—*Jeremiah 27:9*
Do not listen to mediums—*Leviticus 19:31; Isaiah 8:19*
Do not practice fortune-telling—*Leviticus 19:26; Deuteronomy 18:10-11; Micah 5:12*
Do not try to see the future in constellations—*Isaiah 47:13; Jeremiah 10:2*
Egyptian secret arts—*Exodus 7:11,22; 8:7,18*
Egyptian mediums and psychics—*Isaiah 19:3*
Command to execute mediums, psychics—*Exodus 22:18; Leviticus 20:27*
Paul drives a spirit out of a fortune-teller—*Acts 16:16-18*
Occult books burned—*Acts 19:19*
Josiah killed mediums and psychics—*2 Kings 23:24*
Magicians and sorcerers stood before king—*Daniel 2:2*
Saul consults the medium at Endor—*1 Samuel 28:7; 1 Chronicles 10:13*
Cup used for divination—*Genesis 44:2,5*
Wizards—*1 Samuel 28:3*
See Occultism

Dragon

Satan called a dragon and a serpent—*Revelation 20:2*

Serpent alludes to Garden of Eden—*Genesis 3; 2 Corinthians 11:3; 1 Timothy 2:14*

Destined for the lake of fire—*Revelation 20:10*

See Satan

EARTH, DESTRUCTION OF

Earth and sky flee from God's presence—*Revelation 20:11*

Earth staggers like drunkard—*Isaiah 24:20*

Earth will wear out like clothing—*Isaiah 51:6*

The end of the world—*Matthew 24:3,14*

Heaven and earth will disappear—*Matthew 24:35; Revelation 21:1*

See New Heavens and New Earth

EARTHQUAKE

Freed prisoners—*Acts 16:26*

Rolled stone from Christ's tomb—*Matthew 28:2*

Predicted—*Matthew 24:7; Mark 13:8; Luke 21:11*

Will destroy Israel's enemies—*Ezekiel 38:19-20*

Worst in human history—*Revelation 16:18*

Mount of Olives will split apart—*Zechariah 14:4*

Mount Sinai—*Exodus 19:18; Hebrews 12:26*

Sixth seal judgment—*Revelation 6:12*

Will kill thousands—*Revelation 11:13* ·

ELECT

Elect from all eternity—*2 Timothy 1:9*

Father gave certain ones to Christ—*John 6:37; 17:2,6,9*

God calls some individuals before they are born—*Jeremiah 1:5; Galatians 1:15*

God chose Jacob rather than Esau—*Romans 9:10-16*

God's election is loving—*Ephesians 1:4-11*

No one comes to Christ unless the Father draws him—*John 6:44*

Salvation is by grace alone—*Acts 5:31; 11:18; Romans 12:3; Ephesians 2:8-10; 2 Timothy 2:25*

Salvation originates in God's choice—*Ephesians 1:5-8; 2:8-10*

Those appointed to eternal life believe—*Acts 13:48*

Election compatible with God's sovereignty— *Proverbs 19:21; Jeremiah 10:23*

Election glorifies God—*Ephesians 1:12-14*

Election inspires godly living—*Colossians 3:12; 2 Thessalonians 2:13; 1 Peter 2:9*

Election necessary in light of man's depravity—*Job 14:1; Jeremiah 13:11; Romans 3:10-20*

Election necessary in light of man's inability—*Ephesians 2:1*

See Salvation

END TIMES

See Last Days

EPHESUS

Paul stayed there three years—*Acts 19*

Timothy was pastor there—*1 Timothy 1:3,18*

One of seven churches addressed by Christ—*Revelation 2:1-7*

Commended for not going along with evil—*Revelation 2:2*

Commended for testing and standing against false apostles—*Revelation 2:2*

Chastised for abandoning first love—*Revelation 2:4*

Called to repent and do the first works—*Revelation 2:5*

Commended for hating works of Nicolaitans—*Revelation 2:6*

See Nicolaitans

ESCHATON

Dawning of final days—*Acts 2:17; see also Joel 2:28-32*

God's final salvation of His people—*Isaiah 48:20; 49:6; Hosea 3:5*

God destroys His enemies—*Jeremiah 23:20; 30:24*

ETERNAL LIFE

Promised before the beginning of time—*Titus 1:1-3*

Assurance of—*John 10:28-29; 2 Corinthians 5:1; 1 John 5:13*

Available to those who believe in Christ—*John 3:15-16; 5:24; 6:40,47; 12:25*

Starts now and continues into eternity—*John 3:15-16,36; 5:24; 6:27; 17:3; 1 John 5:13*

Believers will never perish—*John 3:16-17; 10:28*

Cannot be inherited by works—*Mark 10:17; 3:10-19*

Christ is eternal life—*1 John 1:2; 1 John 5:20*

Eternal life is in the Son—*1 John 5:11-13*

Eternal life is knowing God and Jesus Christ—*John 17:3*

Eternal glory awaits us—*2 Corinthians 4:17-18; 5:1*

Eternal life and Christ's word—*John 5:24-25*

Eternal life and sowing to please the Spirit—*Galatians 6:8*

Eternal life and leaving things in this life—*Matthew 19:29*

A gift of God—*Romans 6:23*

Given by Christ—*John 6:27,68; 10:28; Romans 5:21; 6:23; 2 Timothy 1:10; 1 John 5:11*

Given by God—*Psalm 133:3; John 17:2; Romans 6:23*

Loving this life and losing eternal life—*John 12:25*

Life forever—*Psalms 21:4; 121:8*

Living water wells up to eternal life—*John 4:14*

Resurrection of the righteous and the wicked—*Daniel 12:2; Acts 24:15*

Promises of—*1 Timothy 4:8; 2 Timothy 1:1; Titus 1:2; 3:7; 1 John 2:25; Jude 1:21*

Wicked do not have—*1 John 3:15*

See Salvation

Eternal Perspective

Apart from body, at home with Lord—*2 Corinthians 5:8*

Death has lost sting—*1 Corinthians 15:55*

Desire to depart and be with Christ—*Philippians 1:23*

Our inheritance awaits us—*1 Peter 1:4*

Set your mind on things above—*Colossians 3:2*

Constant abiding in Christ—*1 John 2:28*

Faithful stewardship—*Luke 19:13*
Blameless living—*1 Thessalonians 5:23*
Joyful expectation—*Titus 2:13*
Obedience—*1 Timothy 6:14*
Patience—*1 Corinthians 1:7; James 5:7*
Readiness—*Matthew 24:44*
Godliness—*Matthew 24:45-51; 1 Peter 1:13-15; 2 Peter 3:11-12,14; 1 John 2:28*
Perseverance—*Matthew 24:12; 1 Corinthians 1:7-9; 2 Thessalonians 3:5; 1 Timothy 6:12-14; James 5:7-8*
Watchfulness—*Matthew 24:42-44; Mark 13:33-37; Luke 12:35-40; 1 Thessalonians 5:4-6; Revelation 16:15*
Encouraged—*Matthew 24:13-14; 1 Corinthians 15:58*
Purified—*Titus 2:13-14*
The Lord's return is near—*Romans 13:11-12; Philippians 4:5; James 5:8-9; 1 Peter 4:7*
Eagerly await the Lord's return—*1 Corinthians 1:7; Philippians 3:20; Titus 2:11-13*
Encourage one another—*Romans 8:23-25; 1 Thessalonians 4:13-15,17-18*
Long for the Lord's return—*2 Timothy 4:8; 2 Peter 3:12; Revelation 22:20*
See Optimism; Watchfulness

Eternal Security

The Lord guards and delivers his faithful ones—*Psalm 97:10*
Depends on Christ's power—*John 10:28*
Depends on Christ's prayers—*Hebrews 7:25*
Depends on Father's power—*John 10:29*
Paul's defense of—*Romans 8:31-39*
Guaranteed by Holy Spirit—*Ephesians 1:13-14; 4:30*
No believers will be lost—*John 6:39*
See God, *Sovereignty*

ETERNAL STATE

All things will be made new—*Revelation 21:5*
Better things await us in eternity—*Hebrews 10:34*
Creation eagerly awaits redemption—*Romans 8:19-21*
Eternal glory awaits us—*2 Corinthians 4:17-18*
The Father's house includes many rooms—*John 14:2-3*
Our inheritance awaits us—*1 Peter 1:3-4*
The new heaven and new earth—*Revelation 21:1,4*
No more curse, no more night—*Revelation 22:3-5*
Our resurrection bodies will live forever—*2 Corinthians 5:1*
We will shine—*Daniel 12:3*
See Heaven; Hell

ETERNITY

Election from all eternity—*Ephesians 1:4; 2 Timothy 1:9*
Eternal God—*Isaiah 44:6; 57:15*
Eternal preparation—*1 Corinthians 2:9-10*
Awareness of—*2 Corinthians 4:18; 5:1-10; see also Eternal Perspective*
Eternity of eternities—*Revelation 1:18*
God inhabits eternity—*Isaiah 57:15*
God is from eternity to eternity—*Isaiah 43:13*
God puts eternity in human hearts—*Ecclesiastes 3:11*
God's eternal existence—*Revelation 1:8*
God's plan from beginning of time—*Ephesians 3:11; 2 Timothy 1:8-10*
Jesus is from eternity past—*Micah 5:2*
See Time

EUPHRATES RIVER

Flowed from Garden of Eden—*Genesis 2:14*
The great river—*Deuteronomy 1:7*

Northern boundary of the promised land—*Deuteronomy 11:24; Joshua 1:4; 2 Samuel 8:3*

Angels bound at Euphrates released during tribulation—*Revelation 9:14*

Will dry up to prepare way for kings from east—*Revelation 16:12*

EVANGELISM DURING THE TRIBULATION

Many conversions—*Matthew 25:31-46; Revelation 7:9-10*

Great harvest will be reaped—*Revelation 14:14-20*

144,000 Jewish evangelists—*Revelation 7; 14*

Two prophetic witnesses testify—*Revelation 11*

EZEKIEL INVASION

Coalition of nations invades Israel—*Ezekiel 38:1-6*

Ancient weaponry—*Ezekiel 38:4*

Animals feast on bodies of enemies—*Ezekiel 39:17-20*

Burial of enemy bodies will take seven months—*Ezekiel 39:11-12,14-16*

Conversion of multitudes—*Ezekiel 39:21-29*

Enemies devise evil plan—*Ezekiel 38:10-11*

Enemies covet Israel's wealth—*Ezekiel 38:11-12*

Enemy weapons gathered and burned—*Ezekiel 39:9-10*

God causes infighting and disease among enemy troops—*Ezekiel 38:21-22*

God controls all nations—*Job 12:23; Psalm 93:1; Isaiah 14:24; 46:10; Daniel 2:20-21; Acts 17:25-26*

God destroys invaders—*Ezekiel 38:17–39:8*

God exalts Himself in His enemies' destruction—*Ezekiel 38:23*

God sends rain, hailstones, fire, and burning sulfur on enemy troops—*Ezekiel 38:22*

God causes earthquake against enemies—*Ezekiel 38:19-20*

God watches over Israel—*Psalm 121:4*

Holy land belongs to Jews—*Isaiah 60:18,21; Jeremiah 23:6; 24:5-6; 30:18; 31:31-34; 32:37-41; 33:6-9; Ezekiel 28:25-26; 34:11-13; 36:24-26; 37; 39:28; Hosea 3:4-5; Joel 2:18-29; Amos 9:14-15; Micah 2:12; 4:6-7; Zephaniah 3:19-20; Zechariah 8:7-8; 13:8-9*

Israel will live in security before the invasion—*Ezekiel 38:11*

Jews will be gathered from many nations—*Ezekiel 36–37; 38:8,12*

No weapon against Israel prospers—*Isaiah 54:17*

Takes place in the "latter years" and "last days"—*Ezekiel 38:8,16*

See Northern Coalition

Faith

Blessed are those who trust—*Jeremiah 17:7*

Cling tightly to faith—*1 Timothy 1:19*

Do not throw away trust—*Hebrews 10:35*

Faith brings answered prayer—*Matthew 15:28; 21:22*

Faith comes from hearing the message through the word of Christ—*Romans 10:17*

Faith is being certain of what we do not see—*Hebrews 11:1*

Faith without works dead—*James 2:17-18*

Trusting God brings joy—*Psalm 40:4*

Live by faith, not sight—*2 Corinthians 5:7*

Miracles through faith—*Matthew 21:21*

The righteous live by faith—*Romans 1:17; Hebrews 10:38*

Small faith yields big results—*Luke 17:5-6*

Tests of faith—*1 Peter 1:7*

Without faith, pleasing God is impossible—*Hebrews 11:6*

Enjoined

Trust in the Lord, not man—*Psalm 118:8*

Trust in the Lord with your whole heart—*Proverbs 3:5*

Be strong and courageous—*Deuteronomy 31:6; Joshua 10:25; Psalm 27:14*

Do not be afraid, for God is with you—*Isaiah 41:10*

Do not worry about your life—*Matthew 6:25; Luke 12:22*

Mustard-seed faith brings results—*Luke 17:6*

Give your burdens to the Lord—*Psalm 55:22*

God will be with you—*Isaiah 43:2*

Trust God, and He will help you—*Psalms 37:5; 62:8; Proverbs 3:5*

The Testing of Your Faith

Faith tested—*Psalm 81:7; 1 Peter 1:7*

Patiently endure testing—*James 1:12*
Brings endurance—*James 1:3*

FAITHFULNESS

Always be faithful—*Proverbs 3:3*
Be a faithful servant—*Matthew 25:23*
Be faithful in prayer—*Romans 12:12*
Choose today whom you will serve—*Joshua 24:15*
Be faithful in small matters—*Luke 16:10*
Faithfulness and the fruit of the Spirit—*Galatians 5:22*
God preserves the faithful—*Psalm 31:23*
The Lord guards the faithful—*Psalm 97:10*
The Lord will not forsake the faithful—*Psalm 37:28*
Hold unswervingly to the hope you profess—*Hebrews 10:23*
Hold firmly to the faith you profess—*Hebrews 4:14*
Hold to the apostles' teachings—*2 Thessalonians 2:15*
Pay attention to what you have heard—*Hebrews 2:1*
Remain faithful even in face of death—*Revelation 2:10*
Stand firm in the faith—*1 Corinthians 16:13*
Stay true to the Lord—*Philippians 1:27*
You must remain faithful—*2 Timothy 3:14*

FALSE APOSTLES, PROPHETS, AND TEACHERS

Wolves in sheep's clothing—*Matthew 7:15-16*
Promote false gods—*Exodus 20:3-4; Deuteronomy 13:1-3*
Deny Christ's humanity—*1 John 4:1-2*
Practice divination and witchcraft—*Jeremiah 14:14; Ezekiel 22:28; Acts 13:6*
Promote immorality—*Jude 4-7*
Influenced by evil spirits—*1 Kings 22:21-22*
Pretend to be sent by God—*Jeremiah 23:17-18,31*
Masquerade as apostles of Christ—*2 Corinthians 11:13-15*
Lie in the name of the Lord—*Jeremiah 14:14*

Utter false prophecies—*Deuteronomy 18:21-22*

Not sent or commissioned by God—*Jeremiah 14:14; 23:21; 29:31*

Encourage legalistic self-denial—*Colossians 2:16-23*

Warnings not to listen to—*Deuteronomy 13:3; Jeremiah 23:16; 27:9,15-16*

Beware of deception—*Ezekiel 34:1-7; Acts 20:28-30; 2 Corinthians 11:2-3*

Beware of false gospels—*Galatians 1:8*

Christ commends those who stand against them—*Revelation 2:2*

Test those who claim to be prophets—*Acts 17:11; 1 Thessalonians 5:21; 1 John 4:1-2;*

Denunciations against—*Deuteronomy 18:20; Jeremiah 8:1-2; 14:15; 28:16-17; 29:32*

Punishment of—*Jeremiah 14:13-16; 20:6; 28:16-17; 29:32; Zechariah 13:3*

FALSE CHRISTS

A different Jesus—*2 Corinthians 11:4*

False Christs will appear in the end times—*Matthew 24:5-26; Mark 13:6-22; Luke 21:8*

FALSE DOCTRINE

Another gospel—*Galatians 1:6-8*

A different Jesus, a different Spirit, and a different gospel—*2 Corinthians 11:4*

Do not be carried away by strange ideas—*Hebrews 13:9*

Do not be deceived by fine-sounding arguments—*Colossians 2:4*

Do not be taken captive through deceptive philosophy—*Colossians 2:8*

Doctrines of demons—*1 Timothy 4:1*

Eve was deceived—*2 Corinthians 11:3*

False prophets—*2 Peter 2:1*

False teachers—*1 Timothy 6:3*

Guard what God has entrusted to you—*1 Timothy 6:20*
Many deceivers are in the world—*2 John 7*
Some have wandered from the faith—*1 Timothy 6:21*
The spirit of Antichrist—*1 John 4:3*
Turning away from truth—*Titus 3:10-11*
See Apostasy

False Prophet

Motivated by Satan—*Revelation 13:11*
Brings deception and false doctrine to the world—*Revelation 13:14*
Controls commerce and enforces worship of Antichrist—*Revelation 13:12,15,17*
Controls religious affairs on earth—*Revelation 13:12*
Performs false signs and miracles—*Revelation 13:13*
Thrown into lake of fire—*Revelation 19:20*
Tormented day and night forever—*Revelation 20:10*
See Antichrist

Famine

Threats to food supply—*Exodus 13:5*
Foretaste of judgment—*Joel 1:15–2:11*
Repentance—*Joel 2:12-17*
Pale horse and rider named "Death"—*Revelation 6:8; 18:8*
See also Leviticus 26:18-20; Deuteronomy 28:23-24; 1 Kings 17:1; Psalm 107:33-34; Jeremiah 8:13; 51:36; Ezekiel 22:24; 30:12; Hosea 13:15; Amos 4:6-8; Nahum 1:4; Haggai 1:9-11

Feasts

Feast of Trumpets may prefigure rapture—*see Leviticus 23:24*
Trumpet at rapture—*1 Corinthians 15:51-52; 1 Thessalonians 4:16-17*

FINAL REVOLT

Some demonic spirits bound in bottomless pit—*Luke 8:31; 2 Peter 2:4*

Satan bound in bottomless pit during millennial kingdom—*Revelation 20:1-3*

Satan loosed at end of millennial kingdom—*Revelation 20:7-9*

Satan judged, cast into lake of fire—*Matthew 25:46; Revelation 20:10*

See Satan; Millennial Kingdom

FIRST AND THE LAST

Jesus is the first and the last—*Revelation 1:17; 2:8; 22:13*

Yahweh is the first and the last—*Isaiah 44:6; 48:12*

See Jesus Christ, *Names and Titles*

FIRST DEATH

For all people (except Christians at rapture)—*1 Corinthians 15:50-55; 1 Thessalonians 4:13-17*

Separation of spirit or soul from body—*Genesis 35:18*

See Death

FIRST RESURRECTION

For believers—*1 Thessalonians 4:16; Revelation 20:4-6*

Second resurrection for unbelievers—*Revelation 20:11-15*

See Resurrection

FOREHEAD, MARK OF THE BEAST ON

Required for buying or selling—*Revelation 13:17*

Invites God's wrath—*Revelation 14:10-11; see also Psalm 75:8; Isaiah 51:17; Jeremiah 25:15-16*

See False Prophet; Antichrist

FOREKNOWLEDGE

God declares the end from the beginning—*Isaiah 46:9-10*

God foreknew His people—*Romans 8:29*
God foretells future, unlike false gods—*Isaiah 42:9; 44:7*

FORTUNE-TELLING

Do not listen to fortune-tellers—*Jeremiah 27:9*
Do not practice fortune-telling—*Leviticus 19:26; Deuteronomy 18:10-11*
Fortune-teller's conversion—*Acts 16:16-19*
Fortune-tellers made fools—*Isaiah 44:25*
No more fortune-tellers—*Micah 5:12*
Tools of fortune-teller—*Isaiah 65:11*
See Occultism

FOUR BEASTS OF DANIEL

Babylon (lion)—*Daniel 7:4*
Medo-Persia (bear)—*Daniel 7:5; see also Isaiah 13:17-18*
Greece (leopard)—*Daniel 7:6*
Rome (beast with ten horns)—*Daniel 7:7*
See Roman Empire, Future

FOUR HORSEMEN OF THE APOCALYPSE

White horse: apparently Antichrist—*Revelation 6:2; see also Daniel 9:26*
Red horse: bloodshed, sword, and war—*Revelation 6:3-4; see also Matthew 24:6-7*
Black horse: famine and death—*Revelation 6:5-6*
Pale horse: massive death toll—*Revelation 6:7-8*

FULLNESS OF THE GENTILES

Gentiles predominate people of God until Israel's conversion—*Romans 11:25-26*
Israel's conversion at the end of the tribulation—*Romans 9–11*

GEHENNA

New Testament word for hell—*Matthew 10:28; see also 2 Kings 23:10; 2 Chronicles 28:3; 33:6; Jeremiah 7:31-34; 32:35; Matthew 5:22,29-30; 18:9; 23:15; 23:33; Mark 9:43-47*
See Hell

GENERATION, THIS

Will not pass away (Matthew 24:34) until these things appear:
Abomination of desolation—*Matthew 24:15*
Great tribulation—*Matthew 24:21*
Sign of Son of Man in heaven—*Matthew 24:30*

GENTILES, TIMES OF THE

Gentile domination of Jerusalem—*Luke 21:24*
Lasts into the tribulation—*Revelation 11:2*

GLORIFICATION

Appearing with Christ in glory—*Colossians 3:4*
Crowns of glory—*2 Timothy 4:8; 1 Peter 5:4*
Certainty for believers—*Romans 8:30; 1 Peter 1:4-5*
Christ glorified in His people—*2 Thessalonians 1:9-10*
Clothed with heavenly bodies—*2 Corinthians 5:1-9*
Death will be defeated—*1 Corinthians 15:51-57; 1 Thessalonians 4:15-17*
Final feature of redemption—*Romans 13:11*
Blamelessness—*1 Corinthians 1:8; 1 Thessalonians 3:13; 5:23*
Future perfection—*Colossians 1:22*
Described—*Philippians 3:20-21; 1 John 3:2*
Inheritance—*Colossians 1:12; 3:23-24*
Resurrected bodily—*Romans 8:23; Philippians 3:20-21*

Salvation will be completed—*Hebrews 9:27-28; 1 Peter 1:3-5*
Share in Christ's glory—*Colossians 3:4*
Transformed to the likeness of Christ—*1 John 3:2*
Glorified with Christ—*Romans 8:17*
Shine—*Matthew 13:43*
See Heaven

Glorious Appearing
See Second Coming of Christ

God

Omniscience
Counts and names all stars—*Psalm 147:4-5*
Sees all things—*Hebrews 4:13*
Knows all about us—*Psalm 139:1-4*
Knows all outcomes—*Matthew 11:21*
Knows all things—*1 John 3:20*
Knows secrets of the heart—*Psalm 44:21*
No one teaches Him—*Isaiah 40:13-14*
Understands every intent of the thoughts—*1 Chronicles 28:9*
Unlimited understanding—*Isaiah 40:28*
Unsearchable in judgments—*Romans 11:33*

Protector of Israel
God battles Israel's enemies—*Exodus 15:3; Psalm 24:8*
Lord of Hosts—*2 Samuel 6:2,18*
Never sleeps—*Psalm 121:4*
No weapon formed against Israel will prosper—*Isaiah 54:17*

Sovereignty
Above all rule and authority—*Ephesians 1:20-22*
Can do all things—*Job 42:2*
Enthroned over all—*Isaiah 40:21-26*

Eternal dominion—*Daniel 4:34-35*
Every knee will bow—*Romans 14:11*
God Almighty reigns—*Psalm 93:1; Revelation 19:6*
His plans alone stand—*Psalm 33:8-11; Isaiah 46:10*
His sovereignty rules over all—*Psalm 103:19*
King over the earth—*Psalm 47:2*
Does whatever He pleases—*Psalm 135:6*
Enthroned as King forever—*Psalm 29:10*
God in heaven above and earth below—*Deuteronomy 4:39; Acts 17:24*
Most High over all the earth—*Psalm 83:18*
No one delivers from God's power—*Deuteronomy 32:39*
Potter rules over clay—*Isaiah 45:9-10*
Rules all nations—*2 Chronicles 20:6*
Rules forever—*Exodus 15:18; Psalm 9:7; Revelation 1:6*
Rules over all things—*Deuteronomy 10:14; 1 Chronicles 29:12*
Who can stop God?—*Job 9:12*
Who can resist God's will?—*Romans 9:19*

Providential Control
Controls bondage in prisons—*Acts 12:7-11*
Controls fish—*Jonah 1:17*
Controls governments—*Romans 13:1*
Controls kings—*Proverbs 21:1*
Controls nations—*Psalm 22:28*
Controls one before birth—*Psalm 139:15-16; Jeremiah 1:5*
Works all things for believers' good—*Romans 8:28*
Protects against overwhelming temptation—*1 Corinthians 10:13*
Provides for animals—*Matthew 6:26*

Sovereign Decree, or Plan
Declares the end from the beginning—*Isaiah 46:10*
Includes building the church—*Matthew 16:18*

Includes final victory—*1 Corinthians 15:23-28*
Includes Jesus' death on cross—*Acts 2:23*
Plan of salvation formed before foundation of world—*1 Peter 1:20*
Sovereign plan for Israel—*Romans 9–11*
Works out His sovereign purpose—*Ephesians 1:11*
See Foreknowledge; Judgment

GOG

Leader of end-times military invasion into Israel—*Ezekiel 38–39*
Prince of Rosh, Meshech, and Tubal—*Ezekiel 38:2*

Not the Antichrist

GOG	ANTICHRIST
leads coalition against Israel (Ezekiel 38:1-6)	leads revived Roman empire (Daniel 2; 7)
time on center stage is short-lived (Ezekiel 39)	leads during much of the tribulation (Revelation 4–18)

GOMER

Mentioned in table of nations—*Genesis 10:2-3*
Member of end-times coalition that invades Israel—*Ezekiel 38:1-6*
Son of Japheth—*1 Chronicles 1:5-6*
See Ezekiel Invasion; Northern Coalition

GOSPEL OF THE KINGDOM

Proclaimed throughout whole world—*Matthew 24:14*
May be proclaimed by 144,000 Jewish converts *(Revelation 7; 14)* and two prophetic witnesses *(Revelation 11)*
Many will respond—*Revelation 7:9-10*

GREAT TRIBULATION

Last three and a half years of tribulation, following abomination of desolation—*Matthew 24:15*

Worst tribulation ever to fall on mankind—*Matthew 24:21*

GREAT WHITE THRONE JUDGMENT

Condemnation—*Matthew 12:36-37*

Degrees of punishment—*Matthew 10:15; 16:27; Luke 12:47-48; Revelation 20:12-13; 22:12*

Destruction—*Philippians 1:28*

Eternal punishment—*Matthew 25:46*

Judgment of unbelievers—*Revelation 20:11-15*

Judgment on basis of works—*Revelation 20:12-13; see also 2:23; 11:18; 14:13; 22:12*

Participants are resurrected unto judgment—*John 5:28-29*

Separation from God's presence—*2 Thessalonians 1:8-9*

Trouble and distress—*Romans 2:9*

Weeping and gnashing of teeth—*Matthew 13:41-42*

White often symbolizes holiness and purity—*Revelation 1:14; 3:4-5; 4:4; 6:11; 7:9,13-14; 14:14; 19:11,14*

See Hell, *Degrees of Punishment*

HABAKKUK, BOOK OF

Wrestled with why good people suffer—*Habakkuk 1:1-11*
Wicked destroyed; believers blessed—*Habakkuk 1:12–2:20*
The earth will be filled with knowledge of the Lord—*Habakkuk 2:14; see also Numbers 14:21; Psalm 72:19; Isaiah 6:3; 11:9*

HADES

General word for place of dead—*Matthew 11:23; 16:18; Luke 10:15; 16:22-23; Acts 2:27,31; Revelation 1:18; 6:8; 20:13-14*
Rich man suffered in Hades—*Luke 16:19-31*
Christ not abandoned to Hades—*Acts 2:27,31*
Jesus holds keys of Hades—*Revelation 1:18*
Hades will give up dead for judgment—*Revelation 20:13*
Hades will be thrown into lake of fire—*Revelation 20:14*

HAGGAI, BOOK OF

Urged returned exiles to rebuild temple—*Haggai 1–2*
Cosmic disturbances in end times—*Haggai 2:6; see also Matthew 24:29-30*

HARLOT, GREAT

See Prostitute, Great

HEALING OF NATIONS

Leaves on tree of life bring healing to nations—*Revelation 22:2; see also Genesis 2:9; Revelation 2:7; 22:14,19*
See Millennial Kingdom

HEAVEN

All things new—*Revelation 21:5*
Treasure in—*Matthew 6:20; Luke 12:33*
Better and lasting possession—*Hebrews 10:34*
Blessing of heaven—*Revelation 22:1-5*

City of glory—*Revelation 21:23*
Created by God—*Genesis 1:1; Revelation 10:6*
Eternal inheritance—*Hebrews 9:15*
Everlasting service—*Revelation 22:3*
Better than earth—*2 Corinthians 5:8; Philippians 1:23*
Father's house—*John 14:1-4*
Glorious anticipation of—*Psalm 45:1-17*
God is Lord of—*Daniel 5:23; Matthew 11:25*
God reigns in—*Psalms 11:4; 135:6; Daniel 4:35*
God's throne—*Isaiah 66:1; Acts 7:49*
Heavenly homeland—*Hebrews 11:13-16*
High—*Psalm 103:11; Isaiah 57:15*
Holy—*Deuteronomy 26:15; Psalm 20:6; Isaiah 57:15*
Holy city—*Revelation 21:1-2*
Home of righteousness—*2 Peter 3:13*
Immeasurable—*Jeremiah 31:37*
Inheritance of believers—*Romans 8:16-17; Galatians 3:18; Ephesians 1:13-14,18; 3:6; James 2:5; 1 Peter 1:3-4; Revelation 21:6-7*
Jesus ascended to—*Mark 16:19*
Jesus preparing place for us—*John 14:1-3*
Kingdom of light—*Colossians 1:12; see also John 8:12*
Kingdom that cannot be shaken—*Hebrews 12:28*
New heaven and new earth—*2 Peter 3:13*
No night—*Revelation 21:25*
Paradise of God—*2 Corinthians 12:2-4; Revelation 2:7*
Paul assured of going to—*2 Timothy 4:18*
People from all races go to heaven—*Revelation 7:9*
Perfect knowledge—*1 Corinthians 13:9-12*
Reward—*Matthew 5:12; Mark 10:21; Luke 18:22; 1 Peter 1:3-4*
Joy—*1 Thessalonians 2:19-20*
Fellowship with God—*Revelation 21:3,7,22*
Light—*Revelation 21:23; 22:5*

Newness—*Revelation 21:5*
Huge—*Revelation 21:16*
Unrestricted access—*Revelation 21:25*

Benefits of Heaven

Christlikeness—*Romans 8:29; Ephesians 5:25-27; 1 John 3:2*
Moral purity—*Philippians 3:20-21; Revelation 21:27*
Perfection—*Revelation 22:3*
Happiness—*Revelation 7:16-17*
Wealth—*Revelation 21:18-21*
No fear—*Revelation 21:12*
No sinners—*Revelation 21:8*
No tears, death, sorrow, crying, or pain—*Revelation 21:4*
No curse—*Revelation 22:3*
Inconceivably wonderful—*1 Corinthians 2:9; 2 Corinthians 4:17*
Divine sustenance—*Luke 14:15; 22:29-30; Revelation 2:17*
Water of life—*Revelation 21:6; 22:1-2*
Tree of life—*Revelation 2:7*
Glorified body—*2 Corinthians 5:1-5; Philippians 3:20-21*
Immortality—*1 Corinthians 15:53-54; 2 Timothy 1:10; Revelation 2:11*
Intimate fellowship with God and Christ—*Isaiah 60:19-20; John 12:26; 14:3; 17:24; 2 Corinthians 5:6-7; Philippians 1:23; 1 Thessalonians 4:17; Revelation 3:4-5,12; 19:6-9*
Physical well-being—*Isaiah 33:24; Revelation 21:4; 22:2*

Promise of Heaven

Those who are righteous—*Matthew 24:34-40,46*
Those who are spiritually minded—*Galatians 6:8*
Those who die to sin—*Matthew 18:8-9; Romans 6:8-11; 2 Timothy 2:11*
Those who endure—*Matthew 10:22; 2 Timothy 2:10-12*
Those who follow Christ—*Matthew 10:37-39; 19:28-29; John 12:26; Revelation 14:4-5*

Those who have been redeemed—*Revelation 22:14*
Those who love God—*James 1:12*
Those who obey God—*Matthew 19:16-17; John 12:47-48,50*
Those who overcome—*Revelation 2:7,11,17; 3:5,12,21; 21:2,7*
Those who persevere—*Romans 2:7*
Those who repent—*Acts 11:18*
Those who seek godliness—*1 Timothy 4:8*
Those who serve God—*Romans 6:22*

HEAVENS, THREE

First heaven is the earth's atmosphere—*Job 35:5*
Second heaven is the stellar universe—*Genesis 1:17; Deuteronomy 17:3*
Third heaven is the "heaven of heavens" and the "highest heaven"—*1 Kings 8:27; 2 Chronicles 2:6*
Paul saw the third heaven—*2 Corinthians 12:2*

HEBREWS, BOOK OF

Book of Hebrews: "Word of exhortation"—*Hebrews 13:22*
Christ, our once-for-all sacrifice—*Hebrews 7–9*
Cosmic disturbances during tribulation—*Hebrews 12:26; see also Revelation 6:12; 8:5; 11:13,19; 16:18*
Heaven, a "better country"—*Hebrews 11:16*
Humans die once and then face judgment—*Hebrews 9:27; see also 1 Corinthians 3:1-15; 2 Corinthians 5:10; Revelation 20:11-13*
Jesus is greater than all Old Testament institutions—*Hebrews 1:5–7:28*
Millennial kingdom is not ruled by angels—*Hebrews 2:5; see also Revelation 20:6*
Warnings against apostasy—*Hebrews 6:4-6; 10:34-36*

HEIRS

All believers—*Romans 4:13; Galatians 3:29; Ephesians 1:11; Colossians 1:12*

Inherit eternal salvation—*Titus 3:7*

Joint heirs with Christ—*Romans 8:17*

Promise of inheritance—*Hebrews 6:12; 9:15; 1 Peter 1:4*

Spiritual blessing—*Galatians 3:29; 4:28*

See Rewards

HELL

Better to lose one part of body than go to hell—*Matthew 5:29-30; 18:9*

Body and soul suffer in—*Matthew 5:29; 10:28*

Penalty for cursing others—*Matthew 5:22*

Destruction—*Matthew 7:13*

Eternal fire—*Matthew 18:8*

Eternal punishment—*Matthew 25:46*

Everlasting—*Matthew 12:32; Mark 9:47-48; 2 Thessalonians 1:8-9; Revelation 14:11; 20:10*

Exclusion from God's presence—*Matthew 25:31-33,41-46; Luke 13:24-28; 2 Thessalonians 1:8-9*

Fiery furnace—*Matthew 13:42; 25:41; Mark 9:47-48*

Fiery lake of burning sulfur—*Revelation 19:20*

Gloomy dungeons—*2 Peter 2:4*

Jewish leaders won't escape—*Matthew 23:33*

Lake of fire—*Revelation 20:13-15*

Not part of original creation—*Matthew 25:41*

Outer darkness—*Matthew 8:12*

Prepared for devil—*Matthew 25:41*

Second death—*Revelation 20:14*

Separation from the righteous—*Matthew 13:47-50; 25:31-33,46*

Suffering—*Matthew 8:12; 10:28; Luke 16:19-31; Revelation 14:9-11*

Torment—*Luke 16:23*

Weeping and gnashing of teeth—*Matthew 13:42*

Occupants of Hell

Beast and false prophet—*Revelation 19:19-20; 20:10*

Death and Hades—*Revelation 20:13-14*

Devil—*Matthew 25:41; Revelation 20:10*

Evildoers—*Matthew 7:19,21-23; 13:38,40-41; 23:29-33; 1 Corinthians 6:9-10; Galatians 5:19-21; Ephesians 5:5; 2 Thessalonians 2:9-12; Hebrews 6:4,6,8; Revelation 21:7-8; 22:14-15*

Lawless one—*2 Thessalonians 2:8*

Unbelievers—*Luke 8:11-12; John 3:18,36; 1 Corinthians 1:18,21-23; Hebrews 3:12-19; 4:1-3; 1 John 5:12; Jude 5*

Degrees of Punishment

Each judged according to what one has done—*Revelation 20:12-13*

God will recompense—*Revelation 22:12*

More bearable for some than others—*Matthew 10:15; 11:21-24*

Repay each person—*Matthew 16:27*

Light and severe punishments—*Luke 12:47-48; Hebrews 10:29*

HINDERER

See Restrainer

HOLY CITY

Jerusalem, the holy city—*Nehemiah 11:1; Daniel 9:24*

Compared with Sodom—*Revelation 11:8*

Heavenly Jerusalem, the holy city—*Revelation 21:1-2,10; 22:19*

See Heaven

HOLY SPIRIT

Removed as restrainer of sin (at rapture)—*2 Thessalonians 2:6-8*

Brings church age to completion at rapture—*1 Thessalonians 4:13-17*

Brings salvation to many during tribulation—*Matthew 25:1-13; Revelation 7:4-8*

Indwells believers—*Jeremiah 31:31-35*

Empowers believers for ministry in end times—*Revelation 7:3-8; 11:3-12; see also Zechariah 4:6; 2 Corinthians 3:5*

Anoints and energizes Christ in the millennial kingdom—*Isaiah 11:1-2*

HOPE FOR THE RIGHTEOUS

Be ready to give a reason for your hope—*1 Peter 3:15*

Be strong and take courage—*Psalm 31:24*

Confident assurance—*Hebrews 11:1*

Everlasting comfort, good hope—*2 Thessalonians 2:16*

Faith and hope in God—*1 Peter 1:21*

God's plans involve hope—*Jeremiah 29:11*

Hope deferred makes heart sick—*Proverbs 13:12*

Hope gives endurance—*1 Thessalonians 1:3*

Hope in God—*Psalms 39:7; 43:5; 71:5; Lamentations 3:24; Acts 24:15*

Hope in God's unfailing love—*Psalm 33:18,22*

Hope in God's Word—*Psalms 119:74,81; 130:5; Romans 15:4*

Hope in the Lord will not be disappointed—*Isaiah 49:23*

Prospect of the righteous is joy—*Proverbs 10:28*

Live in eager expectation and hope—*Philippians 1:20*

Look forward to joys of heaven—*Colossians 1:5*

Those who hope in Lord will renew their strength—*Isaiah 40:31*

Three things endure: faith, hope, love—*1 Corinthians 13:13*

Living hope—*1 Peter 1:3*

See Faith

HOPE FOR THE WICKED

Hope of godless comes to nothing—*Job 8:13*

What hope do godless have?—*Job 27:8*

Wicked are without hope—*Ephesians 2:12*

Wicked will lose hope—*Job 11:20*

Horns

Represent the dominion of kings and kingdoms—*Revelation 12:3; 13:1,11; 17:3-16*

"Ten horns" and "little horn"—*Daniel 7–8*

Horses

Four horsemen of the Apocalypse—*Revelation 6:8*

Jesus at second coming on white horse—*Revelation 19:11*

See Four Horsemen of the Apocalypse

Hour of Testing

Church kept from it—*Revelation 3:10*

God delivers church from the wrath to come—*1 Thessalonians 1:10; 5:9*

New Testament never mentions the church in the tribulation—*Matthew 13:30,39-42,48-50; 24:15-31; 1 Thessalonians 1:9-10; 5:4-9; 2 Thessalonians 2:1-11; Revelation 4–18*

Old Testament never mentions the church in the tribulation—*Deuteronomy 4:29-30; Jeremiah 30:4-11; Daniel 8:24-27; 12:1-2*

See Rapture; Tribulation Period

IMAGE OF THE BEAST

Antichrist proclaims himself as God in temple—*2 Thessalonians 2:4*

Image in temple causes abomination of desolation—*Daniel 11:31; Matthew 24:15*

See Antichrist

IMMINENCE

Judge is standing at the door—*James 5:9*

Lord's coming is near—*James 5:8*

Lord is at hand—*Philippians 4:5*

Events in Revelation will take place soon—*Revelation 1:1*

Lord is coming quickly—*Revelation 3:11; 22:7,12,17,20*

Lord is invited to come now—*1 Corinthians 16:22*

Salvation nearer now than when we first believed—*Romans 13:11-12*

We await God's Son—*1 Thessalonians 1:10*

We await great God and Savior—*Titus 2:13*

We await mercy of Lord Jesus Christ—*Jude 21*

We await revealing of Lord—*1 Corinthians 1:7*

We await revelation of Jesus Christ—*1 Peter 1:13*

We await Savior—*Philippians 3:20*

We eagerly await Him—*Hebrews 9:28*

See also Matthew 16:27-28; 24:3,34; Mark 13:30; Luke 21:28-31; John 14:1-4

See Rapture

IMMORTALITY

Better things await us in eternity—*Hebrews 10:34*

Eternal life—*Matthew 25:46*

Gift of God—*Romans 6:23*
God is my portion forever—*Psalm 73:26*
Hold tightly to eternal life—*1 Timothy 6:12*
Immortality of soul—*Ecclesiastes 12:7; Matthew 10:28; 1 Corinthians 15:54; Revelation 20:4*
Jesus gives eternal life—*John 10:28*
Jesus is the resurrection and the life—*John 11:25-26*
See also Luke 20:36; John 8:51; Romans 2:7; 1 Corinthians 15:53; 2 Corinthians 5:1; 1 Thessalonians 4:17; 2 Timothy 1:10
See Eternal Life; Heaven

INERRANCY OF SCRIPTURE

All God's words are true—*Psalm 119:160*
Every jot and tittle is accurate—*Matthew 5:17-18*
Every word of God is flawless—*Psalms 12:6; 18:30; Proverbs 30:5-6*
God's commands are true—*Psalm 119:151*
God's Word is truth—*John 17:17*
Law of Lord is perfect—*Psalm 19:7*
Jesus overcame temptation with Scripture—*Matthew 4:4*
Jesus overcame trickery with Scripture—*Matthew 22:23-33*
Jesus refers to individual Old Testament words—*Matthew 22:41-46*
Paul refers to individual Old Testament words—*Galatians 3:16*
Ordinances of Lord are sure—*Psalm 19:9*
Scripture cannot be broken—*John 10:35*

INHERITANCE

From God—*Ephesians 1:11*
Christ's treasures—*Romans 8:17*
Eternal life—*Titus 3:7*
Cannot spoil, perish, or fade—*1 Peter 1:3-5*
See Rewards

INSPIRATION OF SCRIPTURE

All Scripture is inspired—*2 Timothy 3:16*

Christ spoke through Paul—*2 Corinthians 13:2-3*

Fulfilled Old Testament prophecies prove inspiration—*Matthew 11:10; 26:23-24,31,53-56; Mark 9:12-13; Luke 4:16-21; 18:31-33; 21:20-24; 22:37; 24:25-27,44-47; John 5:39-47; 13:18; 15:25; 17:12*

God put words in Jeremiah's mouth—*Jeremiah 1:9; 5:14*

God told Moses what to speak—*Exodus 4:12-16; 24*

Holy Spirit guided apostles into truth—*John 14:26; 16:13*

Holy Spirit moved biblical writers—*2 Peter 1:21*

Holy Spirit spoke through David—*2 Samuel 23:2-3; Acts 1:16; 4:25*

Jeremiah was told to not diminish a word—*Jeremiah 26:2*

Jeremiah wrote God's words—*Jeremiah 30:1-2*

Jesus' view of inspiration—*Matthew 5:17-19; 19:3-9; 22:29-32,41-44; Mark 7:5-13; Luke 16:16-17,27-31; 22:36-37; 24:25-27,44-45; John 10:34-36*

John's view of inspiration—*1 John 1:1-5; Revelation 1:1-3,10-11,17-18; 19:9-10; 22:6-8*

Paul's view of inspiration—*Acts 22:13-15; Romans 16:25-27; 1 Corinthians 2:12-13; 7:10; 14:37; Ephesians 3:2-5; 6:17; Colossians 3:16; 1 Thessalonians 2:13; Titus 1:2-3*

Peter's view of inspiration—*1 Peter 1:23-25; 2 Peter 3:15-16*

Luke's Gospel is inspired Scripture—*1 Timothy 5:18*

Paul's writings are inspired Scripture—*2 Peter 3:16*

Paul wrote at Lord's command—*1 Corinthians 14:37*

Paul's words were God's words—*1 Thessalonians 2:13*

New Testament claims Old Testament is inspired—*Matthew 4:4,7,10; Luke 4:14-21; Acts 1:16,20; 13:32-35; 28:23-28; Romans 9:17; Galatians 3:8; Ephesians 4:8; Hebrews 1:8-9; 2:6-8; 3:7-11; 4:3; 5:5-6; 7:21; 10:15-17; 12:5-6; 13:5; 1 Peter 1:23-25*

Old Testament claims inspiration—*Exodus 4:11-16,29-31; 7:1-2; 19:7-9; 20:1-2; 24:4,12; 25:21-22; 31:18; 32:15-16; 34:27-28; Leviticus 26:46; Deuteronomy 4:5; 5:5-6; 6:1-2,6-9; 18:17-22; 31:19,22; 2 Samuel 23:1-2; 2 Kings 17:13; Nehemiah 9:13-14; Job 23:12; Psalms 19:7-11; 78:5; 99:7; 119:160; 147:19; Isaiah 34:16; 51:16; 59:21; Jeremiah 1:9,17; 30:2; 36:1-2,4,27-28,32; Ezekiel 2:7; 3:10-11; 11:24-25; Daniel 10:18,20-21; Hosea 8:12; Amos 3:8; Micah 3:8; Zechariah 7:12*

Scripture cannot be broken—*John 10:35*

Words of Scripture taught by Holy Spirit—*1 Corinthians 2:13*

INTERMEDIATE STATE

Abraham's bosom—*Luke 16:19-31*

Jesus committed His spirit to the Father—*Luke 23:46*

Stephen prayed for Jesus to receive spirit—*Acts 7:59*

Destiny in intermediate state depends on faith in Christ—*Acts 16:31*

Immaterial part separates from material part—*Genesis 35:18; John 19:30*

Paradise—*Luke 23:43*

Ends at believers' resurrection—*1 Corinthians 15:50-55; 1 Thessalonians 4:13-17*

Spirit returns to God who gave it—*Ecclesiastes 12:7*

Falling asleep—*John 11:11*

Conscious Awareness

Absent from body, at home with Lord—*2 Corinthians 5:8*

Moses and Elijah spoke with Jesus—*Matthew 17:1-4*

Paul desired to depart and be with Christ—*Philippians 1:23*

Rich man and Lazarus—*Luke 16:19-31*

Souls under God's altar—*Revelation 6:9*

Thief with Christ in paradise—*Luke 23:43*

IRAQ

Antichrist's headquarters during tribulation—*Revelation 17–18*

May be among nations that invade Israel in end times—*Ezekiel 38:6,9,15,22*

Not specifically mentioned among nations that invade Israel in end times—*Ezekiel 38:1-6*

See Ezekiel Invasion; Northern Coalition

ISAIAH, BOOK OF

Armageddon and its judgments—*Isaiah 34:1-17*

Blessings of millennial kingdom—*Isaiah 35:1-10; 60:1-22*

Glory awaits the faithful—*Isaiah 2–4; 62–63*

God's love and forgiveness—*Isaiah 54:10; 55:3; 63:9*

God's power, majesty, glory, and sovereignty—*Isaiah 44–45*

God's righteousness—*Isaiah 5:16; 11:4; 42:6,21; 51:6*

Judgment against sin—*Isaiah 13–23*

Judgments of tribulation—*Isaiah 24:1-23*

Millennial blessings extended to Gentiles—*Isaiah 56:1-8*

Triumphs of millennial kingdom—*Isaiah 25:1-12*

Messianic Passages

Virgin birth—*Isaiah 7:14*

Deity and kingdom—*Isaiah 9:1-7*

Righteous reign—*Isaiah 11:2-5*

Vicarious suffering and death—*Isaiah 52:13–53:12*

ISRAEL

Distinct from church—*1 Corinthians 10:32*

See Church, *Distinct from Israel*

In Tribulation

Tribulation is "time of Jacob's trouble"—*Jeremiah 30:7*

Israel to experience purging judgments—*Zechariah 13:8-9*

Israel partially delivered from Satan in tribulation—*Revelation 12:14-17*

Portion of Israel delivered, others martyred in tribulation—
Revelation 7:4-17; 13:5-7

See Tribulation Period

Rebirth of

First worldwide gathering in unbelief (1948 and following)—
Isaiah 11:11-12; Ezekiel 20:33-38; 22:17-22; 36:22-24; 38–39; Zephaniah 2:1-2

Second worldwide gathering in belief (related to millennial kingdom)—*Deuteronomy 4:29-31; 30:1-10; Isaiah 27:12-13; 43:5-7; Jeremiah 16:14-15; 31:7-10; Ezekiel 11:14-18; Amos 9:14-15; Zechariah 10:8-12; Matthew 24:31*

Gathered from many nations—*Jeremiah 16:15; Ezekiel 36:24*

Converts at Armageddon—*Zechariah 12:2–13:1*

Will mourn for Messiah—*Zechariah 12:10; see also Matthew 23:37-39; Isaiah 53:1-9*

Will confess national sin—*Leviticus 26:40-42; Deuteronomy 4:29-31; 30:6-8; Jeremiah 3:11-18; Hosea 5:15*

Spiritual awakening—*Joel 2:28-29*

Towns will be inhabited, ruins rebuilt—*Ezekiel 36:10*

Vision of dry bones—*Ezekiel 37*

Will again be prosperous—*Ezekiel 36:30*

Land promises—*Isaiah 60:18,21; Jeremiah 23:6; 24:5-6; 30:18; 31:31-34; 32:37-40; 33:6-9; Ezekiel 28:25-26; 34:11-13; 36:24-26; 37; 39:28; Hosea 3:4-5; Joel 2:18-29; Amos 9:14-15; Micah 2:12; 4:6-7; Zephaniah 3:19-20; Zechariah 8:7-8; 13:8-9*

J

Jacob's Trouble

Tribulation is "time of Jacob's trouble"—*Jeremiah 30:7*
Details of distress—*Revelation 6–18*
See Tribulation Period

Jeremiah, Book of

Spokesman for God—*Jeremiah 1:5*
Warned Israelites of impending judgment—*Jeremiah 2–35*
Jeremiah's warnings endangered his life—*Jeremiah 36–38*
Judgment fell in Babylonian exile—*Jeremiah 39–45*
Tribulation, time of Jacob's trouble—*Jeremiah 30:7*
Day of the Lord—*Jeremiah 30:8*
New Covenant promises—*Jeremiah 31:31-37*

Jerusalem

Jesus often visited—*Luke 2:22-51; John 2:13; 5:1; 10:22; 12:2*
Jerusalem and temple to be destroyed—*Matthew 24:2*
This destruction ended Israel as political entity—*Luke 21:20*
Israel to be reborn in latter days—*Ezekiel 36–37*
Israel a sore spot in world in end times—*Zechariah 12:2-3*
Invaded by northern coalition in end times—*Ezekiel 38*
God will deliver Israel—*Ezekiel 39*
Jewish temple rebuilt in tribulation—*Ezekiel 40–48; Daniel 9:26-27; 11:31; Matthew 24:1-2,15,27-31*
Antichrist brings temporary peace to Jerusalem—*Daniel 9:27*
Antichrist breaks covenant and makes Jerusalem his throne—*Daniel 11:40-45*
Terrible persecution for inhabitants—*Jeremiah 30:4-7*
Antichrist defiles Jewish temple—*2 Thessalonians 2:1-4*
Prophetic witnesses executed—*Revelation 11:7-11*
Armageddon north of Jerusalem—*Revelation 16:16*

Antichrist and allies come against Jerusalem—*Zechariah 12:1-3*

Jerusalem falls to Antichrist—*Zechariah 14:2*

Christ returns to Mount of Olives—*Zechariah 14:4*

Massive earthquake will split Jerusalem—*Zechariah 14:4-5*

Future glory—*Isaiah 44:26-28; 52:1-10; Joel 2:28–3:21*

In Millennial Kingdom

City of God's presence—*Ezekiel 48:35*

City of holiness—*Isaiah 33:5; Jeremiah 31:40*

City of political rule—*Psalms 2:6; 110:2; Isaiah 2:2-4; 24:23; Micah 4:7*

City of prominence—*Isaiah 2:2-4; Zechariah 14:9-10*

City of prosperity—*Isaiah 2:2; 60:11; 66:12*

City of protection and peace—*Isaiah 40:2; 66:20; Jeremiah 31:6*

City of worship—*Isaiah 60:3; Jeremiah 3:17; Zechariah 8:23*

The New Jerusalem

Christ is building—*John 14:1-3*

Measures 1500 by 1500 by 1500 miles—*Revelation 21:16*

Twelve foundations with names of twelve apostles—*Revelation 21:14*

Twelve gates, with twelve angels at gates—*Revelation 21:12*

Always lighted—*Revelation 22:5*

River of water of life flows down its sides—*Revelation 22:1-2*

See Heaven

Pray for Jerusalem

In the end times, Jerusalem is a sore spot in world—*Zechariah 12:2-3*

Pray for the peace of Jerusalem—*Psalm 122:6*

Israel will eventually recognize the Messiah—*Joel 2:28-29; Zechariah 12:2–13:1; Romans 9:3-4; 10:13-14; 11:1*

JESUS CHRIST

God

Alpha and Omega—*Revelation 1:8; 22:13*

Created everything—*John 1:3; Colossians 1:16; Hebrews 1:10*

Elohim, Mighty God—*Isaiah 9:6*

Equated with the I AM of Exodus 3:14—*John 8:58*

Eternal—*Isaiah 9:6; Micah 5:2*

Father addressed Jesus as God—*Hebrews 1:8*

Final Judge of humankind—*Matthew 25:31-32*

First and the Last—*Revelation 1:17*

Forgives sins (which only God can do)—*Mark 2:5-12*

Fullness of deity—*Colossians 2:9*

God and Savior—*2 Peter 1:1; see Isaiah 43:11*

God the One and Only—*John 1:18*

Great God and Savior—*Titus 2:13*

Has life in Himself—*John 1:4*

Has nature of God—*Philippians 2:6*

One with the Father—*John 10:30*

Image of invisible God—*Colossians 1:15*

Immanuel, God with us—*Matthew 1:23*

Is God—*John 1:1*

Prayed to as God—*Acts 7:59*

King of kings, Lord of lords—*Revelation 17:14; 19:16*

Omnipresent—*Matthew 28:20; Ephesians 1:22-23*

Omniscient—*see Revelation 2–3*

Preexisted creation—*John 17:4-5*

Prophecy of Messiah as God—*Isaiah 40:3; Matthew 3:3*

Raised people from dead—*John 5:21; 11:25-44*

Reflects God's glory—*Hebrews 1:3*

Sinless—*John 8:29*

Sustains universe as God—*Colossians 1:17*

Thomas called Jesus, God—*John 20:28*

Unchanging (immutable)—*Hebrews 13:8*
Worshipped as God—*Matthew 28:16-17; Hebrews 1:6*

Eternal

Everlasting Father—*Isaiah 9:6*
Existed before Abraham—*John 8:58*
Existed before everything else began—*Colossians 1:17*
Existed from the beginning—*1 John 1:1*
Existed long before John the Baptist—*John 1:15*
First and the Last—*Revelation 1:17*
From eternity past—*Micah 5:2*
Glory before the creation—*John 17:5*
Is, was, and is still to come—*Revelation 1:8*

Exalted

Ascended higher than heavens—*Ephesians 4:10*
Crowned with glory and honor—*Hebrews 2:9*
Exalted to God's right hand—*Luke 22:69; Acts 2:33-34; 5:31; Colossians 3:1*
Name above every name—*Philippians 2:9*
Sat down in place of honor—*Romans 8:34; Ephesians 1:20; Hebrews 1:3; 8:1*

Judge

Great Judge is coming—*James 5:9*
Judge of all—*Acts 10:42*
We must all stand before Christ—*2 Corinthians 5:10*
Will expose deepest secrets—*Romans 2:16; 1 Corinthians 4:5*
Will judge the world—*Acts 17:31*

King

Authority over everything—*Matthew 11:27*
Bless the King—*Luke 19:38*
Complete authority—*Matthew 28:18*

Government will rest on shoulders—*Isaiah 9:6*
Heir to David's throne—*Isaiah 11:10; Acts 2:30*
King is coming—*John 12:15*
King of kings—*1 Timothy 6:15; Revelation 17:14; 19:16*
King of the Jews—*Matthew 2:2; John 19:19*
Kingdom not of this world—*John 18:36*
Kingship—*John 18:37*
Powerful dominion—*Psalm 110:2*

Lord

Christ the Lord—*Luke 2:11*
Confess Jesus is Lord—*Romans 10:9*
Do all in the name of the Lord—*Colossians 3:17,23,24*
Every knee will bow before Him—*Philippians 2:9-11*
Grow in knowledge of Lord—*2 Peter 3:18*
Holy Spirit enables us to say, "Jesus is Lord"—*1 Corinthians 12:3*
Hypocrites give lip service to Lord—*Luke 6:46*
Set Jesus apart as Lord in your heart—*1 Peter 3:15*
Lord of lords—*Revelation 17:14*
One Lord—*1 Corinthians 8:6*
We live to the Lord—*Romans 14:8-9*
We preach Jesus as Lord—*2 Corinthians 4:5*

Names and Titles

Alpha and Omega—*Revelation 1:8; 22:13*
Bread of Life—*John 6:48*
Carpenter—*Mark 6:3*
Cornerstone—*Ephesians 2:20; 1 Peter 2:4*
Eternal High Priest—*Hebrews 6:20*
Faithful and True—*Revelation 19:11*
Faithful and True Witness—*Revelation 3:14*
First and the Last—*Revelation 1:17*
God and Savior—*2 Peter 1:1*

God's Chosen One, the Messiah—*Luke 23:35*
God's Messenger and High Priest—*Hebrews 3:1*
Good Shepherd—*John 10:11*
Great God and Savior—*Titus 2:13*
Great High Priest—*Hebrews 4:14*
Great Shepherd—*Hebrews 13:20*
Head of the body, the church—*Ephesians 5:23; Colossians 1:18*
Holy One sent from God—*Mark 1:24*
Immanuel—*Isaiah 7:14; Matthew 1:23*
King of kings—*Revelation 19:16*
King of the Jews—*Matthew 2:2; 27:37*
Lamb and Shepherd—*Revelation 7:17*
Lamb of God—*John 1:29*
Last Adam—*1 Corinthians 15:45*
Light of the world—*John 8:12*
Lion of tribe of Judah—*Revelation 5:5*
Lord—*Mark 1:2-3 (see Isaiah 40:3); Acts 2:21 (see Joel 2:32);
    Philippians 2:11*
Lord and Savior—*2 Peter 1:11*
Lord of lords—*Revelation 17:14; 19:16*
Mediator—*1 Timothy 2:5*
Messiah—*Matthew 1:1; 16:20; Mark 14:61; Luke 9:20; 23:2; John
    1:41*
Mighty God—*Isaiah 9:6*
Passover Lamb—*1 Corinthians 5:7*
Prince and Savior—*Acts 5:31*
Prophet—*Deuteronomy 18:15,18; Matthew 21:11*
Resurrection and the life—*John 11:25*
Righteous One—*Acts 7:52; 22:14*
Ruler of Israel—*Micah 5:2*
Savior—*Luke 2:11,30; Titus 1:4; 1 John 4:14*
Shepherd—*Mark 14:27*
Son of God—*Matthew 26:63-65; Luke 1:35; John 1:49; Acts 9:20*

Son of Man—*Mark 2:28*
Son of the Most High—*Luke 1:32*
Teacher—*John 3:2*
True light—*John 1:9*
True vine—*John 15:1*
Way, truth, and life—*John 14:6*
Wonderful Counselor, Mighty God, Everlasting Father, Prince
of Peace—*Isaiah 9:6*
Word—*John 1:1; Revelation 19:13*

Prophecies Concerning Jesus
See Messianic Prophecies

Prophet
Knows and reveals God like no other—*Matthew 11:27; John 3:2,13,34; 17:6,14,26; Hebrews 1:1-2*
Anointed with Holy Spirit—*Isaiah 42:1; 61:1; Luke 4:18; John 3:34*
Christ as prophet was foretold—*Deuteronomy 18:15,18*
Declared His words were from Father—*John 8:26,28; 12:49-50; 14:10,24; 15:15*
Foretold things to come—*Matthew 24:3-35; Luke 19:44*
Full of wisdom—*Luke 2:40,47,52; Colossians 2:3*

Second Coming
See Second Coming of Christ

JEWS
Descendants of Judah—*2 Kings 16:6*
Descendants of Abraham in country of Judah—*2 Chronicles 32:18; Jeremiah 32:12; 34:9; 38:19*
Distinct from church in New Testament—*1 Corinthians 10:32*
God still has plan for Jews—*Romans 9–11*
Israelites, as opposed to Gentiles—*Galatians 2:14; Titus 1:14*

Jewish confession of faith is the Shema—*Deuteronomy 6:4*

Judaism—*Galatians 1:13-14*

JOEL, BOOK OF

Campaign of Armageddon—*Joel 3:9-17*

God gathers nations for judgment in end times—*Joel 3:2; see also Matthew 25:40,45*

Israel regathered to Palestine in end times—*Joel 3:1; see also Matthew 24:31*

God will pardon Israel's sins—*Joel 3:21*

Messiah's reign in millennial kingdom—*Joel 3:18*

People called to repentance—*Joel 2:12-17*

Swarm of locusts as foretaste of the day of judgment—*Joel 1:15– 2:11*

JOHN, GOSPEL OF

Messiah—*John 1:41; 4:25-26; 11:27*

Future resurrection of believers and unbelievers—*John 5:28-29; see also 1 Thessalonians 4:13-17; Revelation 20:11-15*

Purpose for writing—*John 20:31*

Jesus came from heaven—*John 6:42*

Jesus is Christ—*John 1:20; 3:28*

Jesus is King—*John 1:49; 12:13; 18:33,37*

Jesus is Son of God—*John 1:49; 5:25; 10:33; 11:4,27*

Jesus is Son of Man—*John 3:14-15; 5:27; 6:27,62; 9:35*

Jesus is Teacher—*John 1:38,49; 3:2; 4:31; 6:25; 9:2; 11:8; 20:16*

Jesus is the Lord—*John 4:1; 6:23; 11:2; 20:20; 21:12*

Jesus is preparing New Jerusalem—*John 14:1-3; see also Revelation 21*

Jesus' substitutionary sacrifice—*John 1:29,36*

Jesus is the perfect revelation of God—*John 1:18; 14:9*

JUDGMENT

Coming day of judgment—*Isaiah 2:12-21; Romans 9:28; 2 Peter 3:7*

After death comes judgment—*Hebrews 9:27*

God is the only Judge—*Genesis 18:25; Job 34:17; James 4:12*

Judgment day has been set—*Acts 17:31*

God will judge in righteousness—*Psalms 7:11; 96:13; 98:9; Acts 17:31; Romans 2:1-3,5*

God will judge with equity—*Psalm 96:10*

God will judge justly—*Acts 17:31; Hebrews 2:2-3*

God will judge impartially—*Ezekiel 18:19-20,29; Acts 10:34; Romans 2:5-6,11; Colossians 3:25; 1 Peter 1:17*

God will judge men's secrets—*Romans 2:16*

God will judge good and bad—*Ecclesiastes 3:17*

God will judge whole earth—*Psalm 96:13; Matthew 12:36; Romans 14:10,12*

God will judge the wicked—*Isaiah 63:4-19*

Only God can judge—*Romans 8:33*

Christ will judge believers—*1 Corinthians 3:10-15; 2 Corinthians 5:10*

Jesus is judge of all—*John 5:22; Acts 17:31*

God's wrath falls on wicked—*1 Thessalonians 2:15-16*

Based on truth—*Psalm 96:13; Romans 2:1-2*

Administered by Christ—*John 5:22,27; Acts 10:42*

Every deed judged—*Ecclesiastes 12:14*

Great White Throne judgment—*Revelation 20:12*

Hidden will be disclosed—*Matthew 10:26-27*

It is inevitable—*Jeremiah 44:15-28*

It is thorough—*Jeremiah 17:10; Romans 2:16*

It is universal—*Amos 8:8-9; Matthew 25:31-32; Romans 2:5-6; Hebrews 12:23; 1 Peter 4:5; Jude 14-15; Revelation 20:12*

Judge yourself, and you will not be judged—*1 Corinthians 11:31*

Judgment in family of God—*1 Peter 4:17*

Motivates faith—*Isaiah 28:16-17*

Motivates holiness—*2 Corinthians 5:9-10; 2 Peter 3:11,14*

Motivates repentance—*Acts 17:30-31*

Nations judged at second coming—*Joel 3:2; Matthew 25:31-46*

Nothing kept secret from God—*Hebrews 4:13*

Predicted in Old Testament—*1 Chronicles 16:33; Psalms 9:7; 96:13; Ecclesiastes 3:17*

Time set for judgment—*Psalm 75:2*

According to Works

God gives what is due—*1 Corinthians 4:5*

Judgment according to deeds—*1 Peter 1:17; Revelation 20:12*

Judgment according to what people have done—*Psalm 62:12; Proverbs 24:12*

People will be paid back for wrong—*Colossians 3:25*

People will get what they deserve—*Proverbs 11:31*

Reward according to work—*1 Corinthians 3:8*

Parables About the Last Judgment

Parable of the net—*Matthew 13:47-50*

Parable of the sheep and goats—*Matthew 25:31-46*

Parable of the weeds—*Matthew 13:24-30,36-43*

See Judgment Seat of Christ; Great White Throne Judgment

Of Fallen Angels

Eternal fire prepared for devil and his angels—*Matthew 25:41*

Satan and demons cast into lake of fire at the end of the millennium—*Matthew 25:41; Revelation 20:10*

Satan was cast from original position of privilege in heaven—*Ezekiel 28:16*

Satan was judged at cross—*John 12:31; Colossians 2:15; Hebrews 2:14*

Satan was judged in Garden of Eden—*Genesis 3:14-15*

Satan cast from heaven in middle of tribulation—*Revelation 12:13*

Satan bound during Christ's millennial kingdom—*Revelation 20:10*

Some fallen angels now in chains for heinous sin—*Jude 6*

Some fallen angels now in gloomy darkness, held for judgment—*2 Peter 2:4*

Of Israel

Gentile nations judged following second coming—*Matthew 25:31-46*

Jewish survivors judged following second coming—*Ezekiel 20:34-38*

Of the Nations

Follows second coming—*Matthew 25:31*

Nations will be gathered and judged—*Matthew 25:31-46*

Sheep separated from goats—*Matthew 25:32*

Righteous enter kingdom, unrighteous enter punishment—*Matthew 25:46*

The judgment of the nations is distinct from the Great White Throne judgment:

JUDGMENT OF THE NATIONS	GREAT WHITE THRONE JUDGMENT
based on treatment of Christ's brothers (Matthew 25:40)	based on works (Revelation 20:12)
involves sheep, goats, and brothers (Matthew 25:32,40)	involves only unsaved dead (Revelation 20:12)
not connected to resurrection	connected to resurrection (Revelation 20:13)
occurs at second coming (Matthew 25:31)	follows millennial kingdom (Revelation 20:11-12)
occurs on earth (Matthew 25:31)	occurs at Great White Throne (Revelation 20:11)

JUDGMENT SEAT OF CHRIST

Believers judged for things done in body—*2 Corinthians 5:10*

Believers must "run" to win prize—*1 Corinthians 9:24-27*

Believers stand before judgment seat—*Romans 14:8-10*

Believers' works tested by fire—*1 Corinthians 3:10-15*

Christ's eyes discern all—*Revelation 1:14*

Incorruptible crown for those who win race of self-control—
1 Corinthians 9:25

Crown of glory for those who faithfully minister God's Word—
1 Peter 5:4

Crown of life for those who persevere under trial—*James 1:12;
Revelation 2:10*

Crown of righteousness for those who long for second
coming—*2 Timothy 4:8*

Each person rewarded according to works—*Psalm 62:12;
Matthew 16:27; Ephesians 6:7-8*

Lord examines mind, heart, conduct—*Jeremiah 17:10; Revelation
2:23*

Lord will bring motives to light—*1 Corinthians 4:5*

Lord will judge words—*Matthew 12:35-37*

Some believers ashamed at Christ's coming—*1 John 2:28*

Some believers lose rewards but are still saved—*1 Corinthians
3:15; 2 John 8*

KEYS OF DEATH AND OF HADES

Jesus has the keys of Death and Hades—*Revelation 1:18; see also John 5:21-26; 1 Corinthians 15:54-57; Hebrews 2:14; Revelation 20:12-14*

KING, MESSIANIC

Angel informed Mary her son would rule—*Luke 1:32-33*

Authority over everything—*Matthew 11:27*

Believers are subjects of the kingdom—*Isaiah 33:17; Luke 22:29-30; Colossians 1:13; Hebrews 12:28; Revelation 15:3; 22:3-4*

Bless the King—*Luke 19:38*

Complete authority—*Matthew 28:18*

David's throne established forever—*2 Samuel 7:16*

Everlasting kingdom—*Daniel 2:44; 7:14; Luke 1:33*

Father installs Son as King in Jerusalem—*Psalm 2:6*

Foretold—*Numbers 24:17; Isaiah 9:7; Jeremiah 23:5; Micah 5:2*

Glorious—*Psalm 24:7-10; 1 Corinthians 2:8; James 2:1*

Government will rest on His shoulders—*Isaiah 9:6*

Heir to David's throne—*Isaiah 11:10; Acts 2:30*

Jesus King of kings, Lord of lords—*Revelation 19:16*

Jesus preached about kingdom—*for example, Matthew 9:35*

King is coming—*John 12:15*

Kingdom not of this world—*John 18:36*

Kingship—*John 18:37*

Magi worshipped the Babe-King—*Matthew 2:1-2,11*

Messiah from tribe of Judah, reign as King—*Genesis 49:10*

Messiah-King will have everlasting dominion—*Daniel 7:13-14*

Powerful dominion—*Psalm 110:2*

Righteous kingdom—*Psalm 45:6; Isaiah 32:1; Jeremiah 23:5; Hebrews 1:8-9*

Shall overcome enemies—*Psalm 110:1; Mark 12:36; 1 Corinthians 15:25; Revelation 17:14*
Spiritual kingdom—*John 18:36*
Supreme—*Psalm 89:27; Revelation 1:5; 19:16*
Universal kingdom—*Psalms 2:8; 72:8; Zechariah 14:9; Revelation 11:15*

KING OF KINGS AND LORD OF LORDS

Jesus is King of kings and Lord of lords—*Revelation 19:16; see also 17:14*
Many crowns on head—*Revelation 19:11-16*
See also Deuteronomy 10:17; Psalm 136:3; 1 Timothy 6:15

KINGDOM OF GOD

Already here—*Matthew 4:17; 11:11-12; 12:28; 18:1-5; Mark 1:15; Luke 17:20-21*
Not yet here—*Matthew 6:10; 25:34; 26:29; Luke 19:11-27; Revelation 20:1-6*
Future kingdom prophesied in Old Testament—*Isaiah 65:17–66:24; Jeremiah 32:36-44; Zechariah 14:9-17*
Kingdom of Jesus Christ—*Colossians 1:13*
Kingdom teaching prominent in Gospels—*Mark 1:15; Luke 9:2*
Kingdom was present in New Testament times because the King (Jesus) was present—*Matthew 5:3; 8:12; 12:28; 19:24; 21:31,43; 25:34; Luke 12:32; John 3:3,5; 18:36; Romans 14:17; Colossians 1:13; James 2:5; 2 Peter 1:11; Revelation 12:10*
Spiritual reign of God—*Matthew 13; Luke 17:20-21; John 18:36*
Spiritual reign over church—*Romans 14:17; 1 Corinthians 4:20; Colossians 4:11; 1 Thessalonians 2:12; 2 Thessalonians 1:5; 1 Timothy 1:17; 6:15; Hebrews 12:28*

KINGDOM OF HEAVEN

Become like children to enter—*Matthew 18:3*
Belongs to children—*Matthew 19:14; Mark 10:14*
Hard for rich person to enter—*Matthew 19:23-24; Mark 10:23*

Keys of kingdom of heaven—*Matthew 16:19*
Kingdom more important than relatives—*Luke 18:29-30*
Secrets of the kingdom of God—*Luke 8:10*

Parables of the Kingdom of Heaven
Growing seed—*Mark 4:26-29*
Hidden treasure and pearl—*Matthew 13:44-46*
Mustard seed—*Mark 4:30-34*
Net—*Matthew 13:47-52*
Talents—*Matthew 25:14-30*
Ten virgins—*Matthew 25:1-13*
Unmerciful servant—*Matthew 18:21-35*
Wedding banquet—*Matthew 22:1-14*
Weeds—*Matthew 13:24-30*
Workers in vineyard—*Matthew 20:1-16*

KNOWLEDGE INCREASED
Knowledge increased in "time of the end"—*Daniel 12:4*
(The "time of the end" is the future tribulation period—*see Daniel 11:35,40.*)

LAKE OF FIRE

Beast and false prophet thrown in—*Revelation 19:20*

Death and Hades thrown in—*Revelation 20:14*

Devil thrown in—*Revelation 20:10*

Sinners thrown in—*Revelation 21:8*

Those not in book of life thrown in—*Revelation 20:15*

Eternal fire—*Matthew 18:8; Mark 9:47-48*

Eternal punishment—*Matthew 25:46; 2 Thessalonians 1:8-9*

Fiery furnace—*Matthew 13:42*

Fiery lake of burning sulfur—*Revelation 19:20; 20:13-15*

Gloomy dungeons—*2 Peter 2:4*

God's wrath is poured out like fire—*Nahum 1:6; see also Deuteronomy 4:24; Jeremiah 4:4; Malachi 3:2*

Not part of God's original creation—*Matthew 25:41*

Second death—*Revelation 20:14*

Torment—*Luke 16:23*

Weeping and gnashing of teeth—*Matthew 13:42*

See Hell

LAMB OF GOD

Jesus is the Lamb of God—*John 1:29,36*

Unblemished—*Exodus 12:5; Leviticus 4:3,23,32; 1 Peter 1:19*

Died on our behalf—*2 Corinthians 5:21; see also Luke 22:19; John 10:15; Romans 5:8; Galatians 3:13; 1 Timothy 2:6; Titus 2:14; Hebrews 2:9; 1 Peter 2:21; 3:18*

Passover lamb is a type of Christ—*Exodus 12:21*

Transfer of guilt to sacrificial lamb—*Leviticus 4:4,24,33*

LAMB VERSUS BEAST

THE LAMB	THE BEAST
slain (Revelation 5:6)	ferocious (Revelation 13:2)
seven horns, eyes, and spirits (Revelation 5:6)	seven heads, ten horns, and ten crowns (Revelation 13:1)
heavenly beings worship Revelation 5:8	men worship beast and dragon (Revelation 13:3-4)
every creature worships Lamb (Revelation 5:13)	most on earth worship beast (Revelation 13:12)
"Worthy is the Lamb" (Revelation 5:12)	"Who is like the beast?" Revelation 13:4
leads to the New Jerusalem (Revelation 22:5)	leads to the lake of fire (Revelation 14:9-10)

LAMPSTANDS

Seven golden lampstands—*Revelation 1:12-13*
Identified as seven churches—*Revelation 1:20*
Jesus stands in midst of seven lampstands—*Revelation 2:1*
See Seven Churches of Revelation

LAND PROMISES TO ISRAEL

Abraham's descendants will be numerous as stars—*Genesis 12:1-3; 13:14-17*
Land promised to Abraham and his descendants—*Genesis 11:31; 12:7*
Parameters of land promises—*Genesis 15:18-21*
Promises passed to Isaac's line—*Genesis 26:3-4*
Promises passed to Jacob's line—*Genesis 28:13-14*
Promises reaffirmed—*Psalm 105:8-11*

Land permanently restored to Israel—*Deuteronomy 30:5; Isaiah 11:11-12; Jeremiah 23:3-8; Ezekiel 37:21-25; see also Isaiah 60:18,21; Jeremiah 23:6; 24:5-6; 30:18; 31:31-34; 32:37-40; 33:6-9; Ezekiel 28:25-26; 34:11-12; 36:24-26; 37; 39:28; Hosea 3:4-5; Joel 2:18-29; Amos 9:14-15; Micah 2:12; 4:6-7; Zephaniah 3:19-20; Zechariah 8:7-8; 13:8-9*

See Israel, *Rebirth of*

Laodicea

One of seven churches addressed by Christ—*Revelation 3:14-22*

Neither cold nor hot—*Revelation 3:15*

"Spit you out of my mouth" (perhaps discipline)—*Revelation 3:16*

Church thought it was rich, but it was poor—*Revelation 3:17*

Jesus urges repentance—*Revelation 3:19*

Jesus stands at door and knocks—*Revelation 3:20*

Overcomers sit with Jesus on throne—*Revelation 3:21*

Last Days

Rebellion and ungodliness—*1 Timothy 4:1; 2 Timothy 3:1–4:5; James 5:3; 2 Peter 3:3; Jude 18*

God will deliver His people from enemies—*Isaiah 13:6-12; Ezekiel 30:3; Joel 2:11,30-31; Amos 5:18-20*

God will fulfill His promises—*Jeremiah 33:14-16*

God will shower His people with blessings—*Isaiah 2:2-4; 25:9; 65:20-25; Jeremiah 50:4-5; Hosea 3:5; Joel 3:1; Zechariah 8:23*

Believers will be resurrected—*John 6:39-40,44,54*

In New Testament, present church age is "last days"—*Hebrews 1:1-2; 1 Peter 1:20*

In Old Testament times, "last days" or "latter days" referred to tribulation—*Deuteronomy 4:30*

(Caution must be exercised in distinguishing "last days" when used of Israel in the Old Testament as opposed to the church in the New Testament.)

See also Genesis 49:1; Numbers 24:14; Deuteronomy 31:29; Isaiah 2:2; Jeremiah 23:20; 30:24; 48:47; 49:39; Ezekiel 38:16; Daniel 2:28; 10:14; Hosea 3:5; Micah 4:1

LAST HOUR

New Testament times included in "last hour"—*1 John 2:18*

John relates "last hour" to presence of false teachers—*1 John 2:19*

See also 1 Timothy 4:1; James 5:3; 1 Peter 4:7; 2 Peter 3:3; 1 John 4:3; 2 John 7; Jude 18

LAST TRUMPET

In Old Testament, trumpet signaled appearance of God—*Exodus 19:16*

Rapture will occur at last trumpet—*1 Corinthians 15:51-52; see also 1 Thessalonians 4:16-17*

(The "last trumpet" [1 Corinthians 15:51-52] is not the same as the seventh angel's trumpet [Revelation 11:15-19].)

LAWLESS ONE

Antichrist is "man of lawlessness"—*2 Thessalonians 2:3; compare with 1 John 3:4*

Speaks arrogant, boastful words glorifying himself—*2 Thessalonians 2:4*

Will lead world in rebellion against God—*2 Thessalonians 2:9-10*

See Antichrist

LIFE, ETERNAL

All who believe in Jesus have eternal life—*John 6:47,50*

Christ gives eternal life—*John 10:28*

Confidence of eternal life—*Titus 1:2*

Death swallowed up in victory—*1 Corinthians 15:53-54*

Death swallowed up forever—*Isaiah 25:8*

Eternal body made for us by God—*2 Corinthians 5:1*

Gift of God—*Romans 6:23*

Eternal life in Jesus—*1 John 5:11*

Hold tightly to eternal life—*1 Timothy 6:12*
Righteous will go into eternal life—*Matthew 25:46*
Rise up to everlasting life—*Daniel 12:2*

LION OF THE TRIBE OF JUDAH

Tribe of Judah is kingly tribe—*Genesis 49:9-10*
Jesus—*Revelation 5:5*
Jesus alone is worthy to open scroll—*Revelation 5:2-4*
See also 2 Samuel 7:12-16; Isaiah 11:1,10; Matthew 1:1
See Jesus Christ, *Names and Titles*

LITERAL INTERPRETATION

Old Testament Accounts Interpreted Literally in Later Passages
Creation account—*Exodus 20:10-11*
Creation of Adam and Eve—*Matthew 19:6; 1 Timothy 2:13*
Fall of Adam and his resulting death—*Romans 5:12,14*
Noah—*Matthew 24:38*
Jonah—*Matthew 12:40-41*
Moses—*1 Corinthians 10:2-4,11*

Parables and Allegories Distinguished from Literal Passages
Parables—*Matthew 13:3*
Allegory—*Galatians 4:24; see also Isaiah 5:1-7; John 15:1-8*
(Jesus showed that parables have specific interpretations—
   Matthew 13:18-23.)

Other Arguments
Jesus rebuked those who did not interpret the resurrection
   literally—*Matthew 22:29-32; see also Psalm 2; 16*
Jesus interpreted prophecy literally—*Luke 4:16-21*
See Messianic Prophecies

Little Horn

Horns represent the dominion of kings and kingdoms—
Revelation 12:3; 13:1,11; 17:3-16

Ten horns (ten nations in the revived Roman empire)—*Daniel 7–8*

Little horn (Antichrist, who gains control over the empire)—
Daniel 7–8

See also 2 Thessalonians 2:3-10; Revelation 13:1-10

See Antichrist

Little Scroll

Angel from heaven had little scroll—*Revelation 10:1-2*

Sweet in John's mouth but bitter in his stomach—*Revelation 10:8-10;* compare with *Psalm 19:9-10*

MAGOG

Mentioned in table of nations—*Genesis 10:2*

Nation in end-times northern military coalition that invades Israel—*Ezekiel 38:1-6*

See Ezekiel Invasion; Northern Coalition

MALACHI, BOOK OF

Day of the Lord—*Malachi 4:1; see also Isaiah 13:6; Joel 2:11,31; Zephaniah 1:14-18*

God's constant and unchanging love—*Malachi 1:1-5*

Judgment at second coming—*Malachi 3:2-4; see also Joel 2:11; Amos 5:18; Luke 21:36; Revelation 19:11-21*

Millennial kingdom, righteousness—*Malachi 4:2*

Sins of the people pervasive—*Malachi 1:6–2:16*

MAN OF SIN

Also called Antichrist and "man of lawlessness"—*2 Thessalonians 2:3; compare 1 John 3:4*

Speaks arrogant, boastful words—*2 Thessalonians 2:4*

Leads world into rebellion against God—*2 Thessalonians 2:10*

See Antichrist

MANSIONS

Comforting message: Jesus is preparing many rooms and will retrieve us—*John 14:1-3*

See Heaven

MARANATHA

Means "our Lord, come"—*1 Corinthians 16:22*

See also Matthew 16:27; 24:42,44,46-50; 25:31; 26:64; Mark
8:38; Luke 9:26; 21:25,27; John 14:3; Acts 1:9-11;
1 Corinthians 1:7-8; Philippians 3:20; 4:5; 1 Thessalonians
1:10; 4:13-17; 5:1-3,23; 1 Timothy 6:13-15; 2 Timothy 4:8;
Titus 2:13; Hebrews 9:28; James 5:7; 2 Peter 3:4; 1 John
3:2; Revelation 1:7; 16:15; 22:12,20
See Eternal Perspective; Watchfulness

MARK OF THE BEAST

Invokes God's fury—*Revelation 14:9-10*
Contrasts with seal of living God—*Revelation 7:2*
False prophet forces it on people—*Revelation 13:16*
No one can buy or sell without it—*Revelation 13:17*
Alternative is persecution or death—*Revelation 13:7,10,15,17*
See also Revelation 16:2; 19:20; 20:4
See False Prophet; Antichrist

MARRIAGE SUPPER OF THE LAMB

Bride (the church) makes herself ready with fine linen (righteous
acts); those who attend are blessed—*Revelation 19:7-9*

MATTHEW, GOSPEL OF

Abomination of desolation—*Matthew 24:15*
Great tribulation—*Matthew 24:21*
Jesus fulfilled Abrahamic covenant—*Genesis 12:1-3; Matthew 1:1*
Jesus fulfilled Davidic covenant—*2 Samuel 7:12-14; Matthew 1:1*
Judgment of nations—*Matthew 25:31-46*
Many allusions to Old Testament prophecy, including Matthew
2:17-18; 4:13-15; 13:35; 21:4-5; 27:9-10
Olivet Discourse—*Matthew 24–25*
Parable of ten virgins—*Matthew 25:1-13*
Sign of Son of Man in heaven—*Matthew 24:30*
This generation will not pass away—*Matthew 24:34*

Meshech and Tubal

Mentioned in table of nations—*Genesis 10:2*
Nations that participate in end-times invasion against Israel—
Ezekiel 38:1-6
See Ezekiel Invasion; Northern Coalition

Messiah

Messiah means "Christ"—*John 1:41*
Born in Bethlehem—*Luke 2:11*
Jesus acknowledged He is Christ—*Matthew 26:63-64*
Jesus warned of false Christs—*Matthew 24:4-5,23-24*
Believing Jesus is the Christ is the primary issue of faith—
Matthew 16:13-20; John 11:25-27; 20:31
Martha recognized Jesus as Christ—*John 11:25-27*
Peter recognized Jesus as Christ—*Matthew 16:16*
Simeon lived to see Messiah—*Luke 2:26*
See Messianic Prophecies

Messianic King

See King, Messianic

Messianic Kingdom

Sudden and catastrophic arrival—*Isaiah 63:1-4; Joel 3:1-2;
Zephaniah 1:12-18; Zechariah 14:1-9; Malachi 4:1-6; Matthew
24:3,27-31*
See also Genesis 49:10; Exodus 19:6; Deuteronomy 17:14-20;
2 Samuel 7:11-12,16-17; Isaiah 9:6; 24:23; 32:1; Jeremiah
31:31-33; Ezekiel 11:23; Daniel 4:22; 7; 9:24-27; Hosea
3:4; Amos 9:11; Micah 4:7-8; Matthew 26:63-64

Messianic Psalms

Royal psalms—*Psalms 2; 45; 72; 110*
Suffering psalms—*Psalms 16; 22; 40*

MESSIANIC PROPHECIES

Old Testament Refers to Christ

Jesus came to fulfill prophets—*Matthew 5:17*
Moses and prophets spoke of Christ—*Luke 24:27*
Moses wrote about Jesus—*John 5:46-47*
Moses, prophets, and psalmists spoke of Jesus—*Luke 24:44*
Old Testament Scriptures speak about Christ—*John 5:39-40*
Scripture is fulfilled in Jesus—*Luke 4:20-21*
Writings of prophets fulfilled in Jesus—*Matthew 26:56*

Specific Prophecies

Anointed with Spirit—*Psalm 45:7; Isaiah 11:2; 61:1*
Ascension—*Psalm 68:18*
Betrayed by friend—*Psalms 41:9; 55:12-14*
Bore world's sins—*Psalm 22:1*
Born in Bethlehem—*Micah 5:2*
Born of virgin—*Isaiah 7:14*
Buried with the rich—*Isaiah 53:9*
Called out of Egypt—*Hosea 11:1*
Cleansed the temple—*Malachi 3:1*
Coming at set time—*Genesis 49:10; Daniel 9:24-25*
Committed Himself to God—*Psalm 31:5*
Crucified with thieves—*Isaiah 53:12*
Deity and kingdom—*Isaiah 9:1-7*
Disciples scattered after crucifixion—*Zechariah 13:7*
Disfigured—*Isaiah 52:14*
Enemies stare at—*Psalm 22:6-7,17*
Entered publicly into Jerusalem—*Zechariah 9:9*
Escape into Egypt—*Hosea 11:1*
Exercises priestly office in heaven—*Zechariah 6:13*
Flesh did see corruption—*Psalm 16:10*
Had a forerunner—*Isaiah 40:3; Malachi 3:1*
Forsaken by disciples—*Zechariah 13:7*

Forsaken by God—*Psalm 22:1*

Gall and vinegar given Him to drink—*Psalm 69:21*

Hands and feet pierced—*Psalm 22:16*

Hated by Jews—*Psalm 69:4; Isaiah 49:7*

Heartbroken—*Psalm 22:14*

Herod kills children—*Jeremiah 31:15*

Immanuel—*Isaiah 7:14*

Intensity of sufferings—*Psalm 22:14-15*

Intercession for murderers—*Isaiah 53:12*

Judge—*Isaiah 33:22*

Killing of children of Bethlehem—*Jeremiah 31:15*

King—*Psalm 2:6*

Light to Gentiles—*Isaiah 60:3*

Line of Abraham—*Genesis 12:2*

Line of David—*2 Samuel 7:12-16*

Line of Jacob—*Numbers 24:17*

Line of Jesse—*Isaiah 11:1*

Line of Judah—*Genesis 49:10*

Lord—*Psalm 110:1*

Meekness—*Isaiah 42:2*

Ministry in Galilee—*Isaiah 9:1-2*

Ministry of miracles—*Isaiah 35:5-6*

Mocked and shamed—*Psalms 22:7-8; 69:7; 109:25*

No broken bones—*Exodus 12:46; Psalms 22:17; 34:20*

Numbered with transgressors—*Isaiah 53:12*

Patience and silence under suffering—*Isaiah 53:7*

Poverty—*Isaiah 53:2*

Priest—*Psalm 110:4*

Prophet like Moses—*Deuteronomy 18:15-18*

Public ministry—*Isaiah 61:1-2*

Reign of righteousness—*Isaiah 11:2-5*

Rejected by Jewish rulers—*Psalm 118:22*

Rejected by His own people—*Psalm 69:8; Isaiah 53:3*

Resurrection—*Psalms 16:10; 22:22*
Rich man's tomb—*Isaiah 53:9*
Ridiculed—*Psalm 22:7-8*
Right hand of God—*Psalm 110:1*
Scourging and death—*Isaiah 53:5*
Seed of woman—*Genesis 3:15*
Silent before accusers—*Isaiah 53:7*
Sit at right hand of God—*Psalm 110:1*
Slain for our iniquities—*Isaiah 53:3-7*
Sold for 30 shekels—*Zechariah 11:12*
Soldiers cast lots for His clothing—*Psalm 22:18*
Spit on and scourged—*Isaiah 50:6*
Stone of stumbling to Jews—*Psalm 118:22; Isaiah 8:14*
Struck on cheek—*Micah 5:1*
Suffered thirst on cross—*Psalm 69:21*
Taught parables—*Psalm 78:2*
Tenderness and compassion—*Isaiah 40:11; 42:3*
Virgin birth—*Isaiah 7:14*
Without deceit—*Isaiah 53:9*
Zeal for God—*Psalm 69:9*

Micah, Book of

Diviners will be disgraced—*Micah 3:7*
Do right, love mercy, walk humbly—*Micah 6:8*
Holy land belongs to Jews—*Micah 2:12; 4:6-7*
Jerusalem will fall—*Micah 4:11*
Ruler is from ancient times—*Micah 5:2*
Ruler to be born in Bethlehem—*Micah 5:2*
The Lord will rule on David's throne in Jerusalem—*Micah 4:1-5*
No more fortune-tellers—*Micah 5:12*
Second coming ends tribulation—*Micah 2:12-13*

MIDTRIBULATIONISM

Argues that the rapture occurs at last trumpet—*1 Thessalonians 4:16-17*

Argues that the seventh trumpet sounds in middle of tribulation, so rapture is in middle of tribulation—*Revelation 11:15-19*

Argues that the church will be delivered from wrath in second half of tribulation—*1 Thessalonians 5:9*

However, since the entire tribulation is characterized by wrath (Zephaniah 1:15,18; 1 Thessalonians 1:10; Revelation 6:17; 14:7,10; 19:2), it makes more sense to say church is delivered from the entire seven-year period (Revelation 3:10).

See Pretribulationism

MILLENNIAL KINGDOM

Christ's earthly 1000-year reign—*Revelation 20:1-3*

Blessings of millennial kingdom—*Isaiah 35:1-10*

Christ anointed and energized by the Spirit—*Isaiah 11:1-2*

Christ crushes wickedness—*Isaiah 2:2-4,9-21; 24:1-13,16-23; 26:20-21*

Christ restores Israel—*Isaiah 25:7-8; 30:26; 51:11-16; 52:1-12; 65:17-19; Ezekiel 36:24-38; 37:1-28; Hosea 2:16-17,19-23; Zechariah 8:1-17; 9:11-17; Romans 11:25-27; Ephesians 3:11-13*

Christ supreme in all the earth—*Psalm 68:31-32; 110:1-3; Isaiah 2:1-2; 52:10; Daniel 2:31-45; Micah 4:1; Habakkuk 2:3,14; Zechariah 14:9*

Glorious kingdom; no more tears or death—*Isaiah 25:1–27:13*

Earth will be filled with knowledge of Lord—*Habakkuk 2:14; see also Numbers 14:21; Psalm 72:19; Isaiah 6:3; 11:9*

Final rebellion and judgment—*Revelation 20:7-10*

Fire will consume rebels surrounding Jerusalem at final rebellion—*Revelation 20:9*

Follows second coming—*Isaiah 66:1-24*

Future aspect of kingdom—*Matthew 6:10; 25:34; 26:29; Luke 19:11-27*

Glorious reign of Christ—*Isaiah 52:7-12*

Glory of Israel—*Isaiah 60:1-22*

God will not rest until Israel is restored—*Isaiah 62:1-12; Jeremiah 30:16-24; Zechariah 10:9-12*

God intends to redeem Israel—*Isaiah 44:1-23*

God will bring salvation to Israel—*Isaiah 52:1-6*

God's throne will last forever—*Hebrews 1:6,11*

Israel cleansed, glory restored—*Isaiah 4:2-6; see also Zephaniah 3:14-20*

Israel elevated—*Isaiah 61:4-11*

Israel restored as wife of the Lord and inherits glory—*Isaiah 54:1-17*

Israel restored, influential—*Isaiah 45:14-25*

Israel to rejoice in blessings of restoration—*Isaiah 35:1-10; Zephaniah 3:14-20*

Israel restored to land—*Jeremiah 30:1-11*

Millennial temple in Jerusalem—*Ezekiel 40–48*

Jesus will rule on throne of David—*Isaiah 9:6-7; Jeremiah 23:5-6; 33:17-26; Ezekiel 36:1-12; Amos 9:11-12; Micah 4:1-5; Zephaniah 3:14-20; Zechariah 14:1-21*

Lord will reign and judge people righteously—*Psalm 96:1-13*

Millennial blessings extended to Gentiles—*Isaiah 56:1-8*

Millennial kingdom to be established—*Zechariah 14:9-21*

Nations will tremble when Lord reigns—*Psalm 99:1-9*

Peace—*Isaiah 19:24-25*

Productivity—*Isaiah 35*

Regathering of Israel promised—*Jeremiah 23:7-8*

Righteous King will reign over Israel—*Jeremiah 23:5-6*

Righteous kingdom—*Isaiah 11:4; Malachi 4:2*

Satan bound during millennial kingdom—*Revelation 20:1-3*

Satan loosed at end of millennial kingdom to deceive nations—*Revelation 20:7-9*

Universal peace and blessing—*Psalm 46:8-9; Isaiah 2:4; 9:5-7; 11:6-9; 35:1-10; 55:9-13; 65:20-25; Hosea 2:18; Joel 3:17-18,20-21; Amos 9:11-15; Micah 4:1-5; Zechariah 9:10-11; 14:6-9,20-21; Ephesians 3:9-20*

Universal rule of King on earth—*Psalm 72:7-11; see also Isaiah 2:1-5*

The Lord's reign brings great joy—*Psalm 98:1-9*

Wine in millennial kingdom—*Matthew 26:27-29; Mark 14:23-25; Luke 22:17-18*

See also Psalm 2:6-9; Isaiah 65:18-23; Jeremiah 31:12-14,31-37; Ezekiel 34:25-29; 37:1-13; 40–48; Daniel 2:35; 7:13-14; Joel 2:21-27; Amos 9:13-14; Micah 4:1-7; Zephaniah 3:9-20

See Jesus Christ, *King;* Second Coming of Christ

Moon

Sun, moon, and stars darkened during tribulation—*Revelation 8:12*

Sun becomes black, moon like blood during tribulation—*Revelation 6:12*

Sun darkened, moon darkened, stars fall, heavens shake at the second coming—*Matthew 24:29-30*

See also Isaiah 13:10; 24:23; Ezekiel 32:7; Joel 2:10,31; 3:15; Amos 5:20; 8:9; Zephaniah 1:15; Acts 2:20

Mount of Megiddo

Location of Barak's battle with Canaanites—*Judges 4*

Location of Gideon's battle with Midianites—*Judges 7*

See Armageddon

Mount of Olives

Location of Christ's return—*Zechariah 14:4*

Messiah's return is to same mountain from which He ascended—*Acts 1:10-11*

See Second Coming of Christ

MYSTERIES

Truths unknown in Old Testament times but now revealed—*Matthew 13:17; Colossians 1:26*

Mysteries of the kingdom of heaven—*Matthew 13:3-50; Mark 4:26-29*

Mystery of bride of Christ—*Ephesians 5:28-32*

Mystery of God—*Revelation 10:7*

Mystery of God, even Christ—*1 Corinthians 2:7, Colossians 2:2,9*

Mystery of godliness—*1 Timothy 3:16*

Mystery of His will—*Ephesians 1:9-11*

Mystery of indwelling Christ in believers—*John 15:4; Ephesians 2:20; Philippians 1:21; Colossians 1:26-27*

Mystery of iniquity—*2 Thessalonians 2:7*

Mystery of Israel's blindness during church age—*Romans 11:25-26*

Mystery of rapture—*1 Corinthians 15:51-52; 1 Thessalonians 4:14,16*

Mystery of seven stars and lampstands—*Revelation 1:20*

Mystery of union of Jews and Gentiles in one body—*Ephesians 3:3-4,9*

Mystery of Babylon the Great—*Revelation 17:5,7*

NECROMANCY
See Occultism

NEW COVENANT
Blessings connected with—*Hebrews 8:10-12*
Fulfilled in Christ—*Luke 1:68-79*
Mediator of—*Hebrews 8:6; 9:15; 12:24*
Brings forgiveness of sin—*Jeremiah 31:31-34*
Sanctifies—*Hebrews 10:29*
Instills a new heart—*Jeremiah 31:33; Hebrews 8:10; 10:16*
Creates a new relationship with God—*Jeremiah 31:33; Ezekiel 16:62; 37:26-27; Hebrews 8:10*
Brings peace—*Isaiah 54:10; Ezekiel 34:25; 37:26*
Includes redemption—*Isaiah 49:8; Jeremiah 31:34; Hebrews 10:19-20*
Removes sin—*Jeremiah 31:34; Romans 11:27; Hebrews 10:17*
Ratified by blood of Christ—*Hebrews 9:11-14,16-23*
In the Upper Room, Jesus spoke of the cup as "the new covenant in My blood"—*Luke 22:20; 1 Corinthians 11:25*
See also Isaiah 59:21; Ezekiel 36:25-27; 37:10-23; Matthew 26:26-28; Romans 8:2; 11:26-27; 2 Corinthians 3:3,6
See Covenants, Biblical

NEW HEAVENS AND NEW EARTH
A regeneration (or renewal) is coming—*Matthew 19:28*
Believers will behold God face-to-face—*Revelation 22:4*
Earth and heaven doomed for destruction—*2 Peter 3:10-14*
Earth now subject to futility—*Romans 8:20*
First heaven and earth give way to a new heaven and new earth—*Revelation 21:1-4; see also Psalm 102:25-26; Isaiah 51:6; Matthew 5:18; 24:35; Hebrews 1:10-12; 2 Peter 3:7-13*
God makes all things new—*Revelation 21:5*

God will wipe away every tear, abolish death—*Revelation 21:3-4*

New heavens, new earth—*Isaiah 65:17; 66:22; Matthew 19:28; Acts 3:21; Romans 8:18-22; 1 Corinthians 15:22-28; Ephesians 1:9-10; 2 Peter 3:13; Revelation 21:1-8*

New Jerusalem comes down out of heaven—*Revelation 21:2*

New Jerusalem indescribably beautiful—*Revelation 21:9-11*

No longer any curse—*Revelation 22:3*

No more death, crying, or pain—*Revelation 21:4*

Physical world will perish—*Hebrews 1:10-12*

Present earth and heaven flee away, destroyed—*Revelation 20:11*

Restoration of all things—*Acts 3:21*

Saints will see God's face—*Revelation 22:4-5*

Satan and sinners quarantined—*Revelation 20:10*

Reflects God's glory—*Isaiah 65:17-25*

NEW JERUSALEM

Christ is building—*John 14:1-3*

Always lighted—*Revelation 22:5*

Measures 1500 by 1500 by 1500 miles—*Revelation 21:16*

River of water of life flows down sides—*Revelation 22:1-2*

Twelve foundations with names of 12 apostles—*Revelation 21:14*

Twelve gates, with 12 angels at gates—*Revelation 21:12*

See Heaven; New Heavens and New Earth

NICOLAITANS

Church at Ephesus was commended for standing against Nicolaitans—*Revelation 2:6,15; see also 2 Peter 2:15; Jude 11*

NOAH, DAYS OF

Second coming as unexpected as the flood—*Matthew 24:37; Luke 17:26*

Noah warned people but was ignored—*2 Peter 2:5*

See Eternal Perspective; Watchfulness

NORTHERN COALITION

Rosh, modern Russia—*Ezekiel 38:3*

Magog, southern portion of former Soviet Union—*Ezekiel 38:2*

Meshech and Tubal, modern Turkey—*Ezekiel 38:2-3*

Persia, modern Iran—*Ezekiel 38:5*

Ethiopia, modern Sudan—*Ezekiel 38:5*

Put, modern Libya—*Ezekiel 38:5*

Gomer, modern Turkey—*Ezekiel 38:6*

Beth-togarmah, modern Turkey—*Ezekiel 38:6*

See Ezekiel Invasion

NUMBER OF THE BEAST

666, number of beast and number of man—*Revelation 13:18*

See Antichrist

NUMBERS IN THE BOOK OF REVELATION

One-tenth—*Revelation 11:13*

One-fourth—*Revelation 6:8*

One-third—*Revelation 8:7,9-12; 9:15,18; 12:4*

One—*Revelation 4:8; 5:5; 6:1; 7:13; 13:3; 15:7; 17:1,10,12-13; 18:8,10,17,19; 21:9,21*

Two—*Revelation 1:16; 2:12; 9:12; 11:3-4,10; 12:14; 13:11; 19:20*

Three—*Revelation 6:6; 8:13; 9:18; 16:13,19; 21:13*

Three and one-half—*Revelation 11:9,11; 12:14*

Four—*Revelation 4:6,8; 5:6,8,14; 6:1,6; 7:1-2,11; 9:13-15; 14:3; 15:7; 19:4; 20:8; 21:16*

Five—*Revelation 9:5,10; 17:10*

Six—*Revelation 4:8*

Seven—*Revelation 1:4,11-12,16,20; 2:1; 3:1; 4:5; 5:1,5-6; 6:1; 8:2,6; 10:3-4; 12:3; 13:1; 15:1,6-8; 16:1; 17:1,3,7,9-10; 21:9*

Ten—*Revelation 2:10; 12:3; 13:1; 17:3,7,12,16*

24—*Revelation 4:4,10; 5:8; 11:16; 19:4*

42—*Revelation 11:2; 13:5*

666—*Revelation 13:18*
1000, 1000s—*Revelation 5:11; 20:2-7*
1,260—*Revelation 11:3; 12:6*
7,000—*Revelation 11:13*
12,000—*Revelation 7:5-8; 21:16*
144,000—*Revelation 7:4; 14:1,3*

Obadiah

Deliverers (judges who rule in millennial kingdom?)—*Obadiah 21*
The day of the Lord—*Obadiah 15; see also Joel 3:2*

Occultism

Astrologers cannot interpret dreams—*Daniel 4:7*
Astrologers cannot save you—*Isaiah 47:13*
Consulting mediums brings judgment—*Leviticus 20:6*
Diviners will be disgraced—*Micah 3:7*
Do not summon spirits of dead—*Deuteronomy 18:10-11*
Do not listen to fortune-tellers—*Jeremiah 27:9*
Do not listen to mediums—*Leviticus 19:31; Isaiah 8:19*
Do not practice fortune-telling—*Leviticus 19:26*
Do not try to read the future in the stars—*Jeremiah 10:2*
Egyptian magicians' secret arts—*Exodus 7:11,22; 8:7,18*
Egyptian mediums and psychics—*Isaiah 19:3*
Mediums and psychics to be executed (in Old Testament times)—*Exodus 22:18; Leviticus 20:6,27*
Fortune-teller—*Acts 16:16,18*
Incantation books burned—*Acts 19:19*
Josiah exterminated mediums and psychics—*2 Kings 23:24*
Magicians, sorcerers stood before king—*Daniel 2:2*
Medium at Endor—*1 Samuel 28:7*
No fortune-telling or sorcery—*Deuteronomy 18:10-11*
No more fortune-tellers—*Micah 5:12*
Reading stars—*Isaiah 47:13*
Saul consulted medium—*1 Chronicles 10:13*
Sorcery and divination—*2 Kings 21:6*
A cup used for divining—*Genesis 44:2-5*
Wizards—*1 Samuel 28:3*

OLIVET DISCOURSE

The days of Noah—*Matthew 24:36-39*
Signs of end of age—*Matthew 24:4-28*
Second half of tribulation—*Matthew 24:15-26*
Great tribulation—*Matthew 24:21*
Abomination of desolation—*Matthew 24:15*
Destruction of Jewish temple—*Matthew 24:1-2*
Parables that stress watchfulness and readiness—*Matthew 24:32-35,45-51; 25:1-13,14-30*
Parables of judgment—*Matthew 25:1-46*
Glorious return of Christ—*Matthew 24:27-31*
Judgment of nations following second coming—*Matthew 24:31-46*
This generation will not pass away—*Matthew 24:34*

OPTIMISM

Be confident—*2 Corinthians 5:6*
Be joyful always—*1 Thessalonians 5:16*
Be strong and take heart—*Psalm 31:24*
Cheerful heart is good medicine—*Proverbs 17:22*
God has plans for us—*Jeremiah 29:10-11*
Hope in God—*Psalm 42:5*
Let us rejoice and be glad—*Psalm 118:24*
Lift up your eyes to the hills—*Psalm 121:1*
No fear of bad news—*Psalm 112:7-8*
There is a future—*Psalm 37:37*
See Eternal Perspective; Watchfulness

OVERCOMERS

Blessing is promised for overcomers in seven churches—*Revelation 2:7,11,17,26; 3:5,12,21*
Overcomers may simply be Christians—*1 John 5:5*
Loss of salvation not implied—*see John 10:28-30; Romans 8:29-39; Ephesians 1:13; 4:30; Hebrews 7:25*
May relate to rewards—*compare with 1 Corinthians 3:1-10; 2 Corinthians 5:10*

Parable of the Fig Tree

Be accurate observers of the times—*Matthew 16:1-3; Luke 21:25-28*

When branch puts forth leaves, summer is near (when signs occur, Christ's coming is near)—*Matthew 24:32-33*

See Eternal Perspective; Watchfulness

Parables of the Kingdom

Growing seed—*Mark 4:26-29*

Hidden treasure and pearl—*Matthew 13:44-46*

Mustard seed—*Mark 4:30-34*

Net—*Matthew 13:47-52*

Talents—*Matthew 25:14-30*

Ten virgins—*Matthew 25:1-13*

Wedding banquet—*Matthew 22:1-14*

Weeds—*Matthew 13:24-30*

Workers in vineyard—*Matthew 20:1-16*

Unmerciful servant—*Matthew 18:21-35*

Paradise

Paul caught up to paradise—*2 Corinthians 12:4*

Thief with Christ in paradise—*Luke 23:43*

Tree of life in paradise of God—*Revelation 2:7*

See Heaven

Parousia

(Greek word meaning "presence" or "coming," used of second coming)

Arrival of king—*Matthew 24:3,27,37,39; 1 Corinthians 15:23; 1 Thessalonians 2:19; 3:13; 4:15; 5:23; 2 Thessalonians 2:1,8; James 5:7-8; 2 Peter 3:4,12; 1 John 2:28*

Lord's coming at rapture—*1 Thessalonians 4:15*

Jesus will return the way He left (physically and visibly)—*Acts 1:11*
Every eye will see Him coming with the clouds—*Revelation 1:7*
Son of Man coming in His kingdom—*Matthew 16:28*
Son of Man is coming—*Matthew 10:23*
Son of Man is coming in Father's glory with angels—*Matthew 16:27; see also 25:31*
See Second Coming of Christ

PARTIAL RAPTURE VIEW

Based on parable of ten virgins: five prepared, five unprepared—*Matthew 25:1-13*

Contradicted by Other Scriptures
All believers are saved—*John 3:16-17; Acts 16:31*
Rapture includes all saved people—*1 Corinthians 15:51-52*
Spirit baptism places all believers in Christ's body—*1 Corinthians 12:13*
All believers will be raptured—*1 Thessalonians 4:16-17*
See Pretribulationism

PATMOS

Place of exile for John, author of Revelation—*Revelation 1:9*

PEACE AND SAFETY

Destruction will fall when people claim peace and safety—*1 Thessalonians 5:1-3*
Illusion of peace and safety when Antichrist signs covenant with Israel—*Daniel 9:27*
Calamity in 1 Thessalonians 5:1-3 is a post-rapture event—*see 1 Thessalonians 4:13-17*
Examples of blindness to impending judgment—*Jeremiah 6:14; 8:11; 14:13-14; Lamentations 2:14; Ezekiel 13:10,16; Micah 3:5*

PERGAMUM

One of seven churches Christ addresses in Asia Minor—*Revelation 1:11; 2:12-17*

Satan's throne in Pergamum—*Revelation 2:12*
Antipas martyred in Pergamum—*Revelation 2:12*
Some held to teaching of Balaam—*Revelation 2:14*
Some fell to sexual immorality—*Revelation 2:14*
Some held to teaching of Nicolaitans—*Revelation 2:15*
Christ urges repentance—*Revelation 2:16*
Overcomers promised blessing—*Revelation 2:17*

PERSIA (MODERN IRAN)

Nation in northern military coalition that will invade Israel in
end times—*Ezekiel 38:1-6*
See also 2 Chronicles 36:20-23; Ezra 1:1-2,8; 3:7; 4:3,5,7,24;
6:14; 7:1; 9:9; Esther 1:3,14,18; 10:2; Ezekiel 27:10; Daniel
8:20; 10:1,13,20; 11:2
See Ezekiel Invasion; Northern Coalition

PETER, 1 AND 2

Day of the Lord coming like thief—*2 Peter 3:10*
End of all things is at hand—*1 Peter 4:7*
Heavens and earth burned up—*2 Peter 3:10*
Imperishable inheritance awaits believers in heaven—*1 Peter 1:4*
Judgment is imminent—*2 Peter 3:7*
New heavens and new earth—*2 Peter 3:13*
Prophecy ought to lead to holiness and godliness—*2 Peter 3:11,14*
Unbelief and scoffers in end times—*1 Peter 3:3-4*

PHILADELPHIA

One of seven churches addressed by Christ in Asia Minor—
Revelation 3:7-13
Obedient to Word of God—*Revelation 3:8*
Christ gives them an open door—*Revelation 3:8*
Synagogue of Satan—*Revelation 3:9*
Rapture promised—*Revelation 3:10*
Christ coming soon—*Revelation 3:11*

Overcomers promised blessing—*Revelation 3:12*
New Jerusalem—*Revelation 3:12*

PLAGUES AND PESTILENCES

Egyptians smitten by plagues—*Exodus 7:14-25; 8:1-15; 9:1-7; 10:21-29*

End-time plagues—*Revelation 6:8; 9:18,20; 11:6; 15:1,6,8; 16:9,21; 18:4,8; 21:9; 22:18*

See also Genesis 12:17; Leviticus 26:25; Numbers 14:12; Deuteronomy 28:21; 32:24; 2 Samuel 24:13,15; 1 Kings 8:37; 1 Chronicles 21:12,14; 2 Chronicles 6:28; 7:13; 20:9; Job 27:15; Psalm 91:3,6; Jeremiah 14:12; 15:2; 18:21; 21:6-7,9; 24:10; 27:8,13; 28:8; 29:17-18; 32:24,36; 34:17; 38:2; 42:17,22; 43:11; 44:13; Ezekiel 5:12,17; 6:11-12; 7:15; 12:16; 14:19,21; 28:23; 33:27; 38:22; Hosea 13:14; Amos 4:10; Habakkuk 3:5; Luke 7:21; John 22:18

See Judgment

POSTMILLENNIALISM

(The view that the world will be Christianized before Christ comes.)

Basis of Postmillennialism

Universal proclamation of gospel—*Matthew 28:18-20*
People from all nations saved—*Revelation 7:9-10*
Christ rules from throne in heaven (not earth)—*Psalms 9:5; 47:2*
Parable of mustard seed indicates continual advance of Christianity in world—*Matthew 13:31-32*

Problems with Postmillennialism

End-times apostasy is predicted—*Matthew 24:3-14; Luke 18:8; 1 Timothy 4:1-5; 2 Timothy 3:1-7*
Scripture promises an earthly rule of Christ—*Isaiah 9:6-7; Jeremiah 23:5-6; 33:17-26; Ezekiel 36:1-12; Amos 9:11-12; Micah 4:1-5; Zephaniah 3:14-20; Zechariah 14:1-21*
See Premillennialism

POSTTRIBULATIONISM

(The view that the rapture follows the tribulation)

All believers resurrected at end of tribulation—*Revelation 20:4-6*

At end of tribulation, one is taken and one is left—*Matthew 24:37-40 (but see Luke 17:37)*

Saints are in the tribulation—*Revelation 6:9-11*

See Pretribulationism for verses that strongly argue against this view.

PREDESTINATION

Father draws people—*John 6:44*

Father gave followers to Jesus—*John 6:39*

God chose us in Christ—*Ephesians 1:4*

God has prearranged a plan—*Acts 2:23*

God set Jeremiah apart from birth—*Jeremiah 1:5*

God's plan is from all eternity—*Ephesians 3:11*

Many are called, but few are chosen—*Matthew 22:14*

Paul chosen before birth—*Galatians 1:15*

Grace given long before world began—*2 Timothy 1:9*

See Elect; Foreknowledge; God, *Sovereignty*

PREMILLENNIALISM

(The view that Jesus will return before the millennial kingdom)

Chronology

Christ's second coming—*Revelation 19*

Then millennial kingdom—*Revelation 20:1-6*

Support for Premillennialism

Land promises to Abraham are unconditional and not yet fulfilled—*Genesis 13:14-18*

Promise of a Davidic ruler is unconditional—*2 Samuel 7:12-16*

Old Testament ends with expectation of messianic kingdom—*Isaiah 9:6; 16:5; Malachi 3:1*

Jesus and apostles will reign on thrones in Jerusalem—*Matthew 19:28; 25:31-34; Acts 1:6-7*

Paul promised Israel will one day be restored—*Romans 9:3-4; 11:1*

PRETERISM

(The faulty view that prophecies of Matthew 24–25 and Revelation were fulfilled in AD 70)

Support for Preterism

"This generation" will not pass till all things fulfilled—*Matthew 24:34*

Some of Christ's followers would not taste death till He comes—*Matthew 16:28*

Events were to take place soon—*Revelation 1:1*

Arguments Against Preterism

No astronomical events in AD 70—*Matthew 24:29*

Third of mankind not killed AD 70—*Revelation 9:18*

Every living creature in sea did not die AD 70—*Revelation 16:3*

Jesus did not return "on the clouds of the sky, with power and great glory" in AD 70—*Matthew 24:30*

"This generation" (Matthew 24:34) probably refers to the tribulation generation, not the first-century generation—*Matthew 24:15-30*

Matthew 16:28 probably refers to transfiguration—*see Matthew 17:1-13*

"Soon" in Revelation 1:1 refers to quick progress of prophecies—*see Luke 18:8 (where the same Greek word means "quickly")*

See Literal Interpretation

PRETRIBULATIONISM

Best explains sudden apostasy that emerges after removal of the restrainer (apparently the Holy Spirit)—*2 Thessalonians 2:3-7; see also John 14:16; 1 Corinthians 3:17*

Christ will bring raptured church to heaven, not remain on earth (contradicts posttribulationism)—*John 14:1-3*

Church delivered out of time of trouble—*Revelation 3:10*

Church delivered from wrath to come—*1 Thessalonians 1:10; 5:9; see also Romans 5:9*

Church not mentioned in long description of tribulation—*see Revelation 4–18*

No New Testament passage on tribulation mentions church—*Matthew 13:30,39-42,48-50; 24:15-31; 1 Thessalonians 1:9-10; 5:4-9; 2 Thessalonians 2:1-11; Revelation 4–18*

No Old Testament passage on tribulation mentions church—*Deuteronomy 4:29-30; Jeremiah 30:4-11; Daniel 8:24-27; 12:1-2*

God protects His people before judgment falls—*see 2 Peter 2:5-9*

PREWRATH RAPTURE

(The view that the rapture precedes God's wrath in the latter part of the tribulation)

Support for Prewrath Rapture

Church will not experience God's wrath—*2 Thessalonians 1:5-10*

God's wrath not unleashed until seventh seal, latter part of tribulation—*Revelation 6:12–8:1*

Arguments Against Prewrath Rapture

All seven seal judgments come from same source: God—*Revelation 6; 8*

Wrath of the Lamb—*Revelation 6:15-16; see also 6:1,3,5,7,9,12; 8:1*

Entire tribulation is characterized by God's wrath—*Zephaniah 1:15,18; 1 Thessalonians 1:10; Revelation 6:17; 14:7,10; 19:2*

See Pretribulationism

PROPHECY

A gift of Holy Spirit—*1 Corinthians 12:10*

Not based on man's will—*2 Peter 1:21*

Certainty of God's Word—*Ezekiel 12:26-28*

End known from beginning—*Isaiah 46:10-11*

God fulfills prophet's message—*Isaiah 44:26*
Is a sure word—*2 Peter 1:19*
Prime purpose of prophecy—*John 13:19*
Prophetic visions and dreams—*Numbers 12:6*
Qualification for a prophet—*1 Samuel 10:12*

Rooted in God
God declares things before they occur—*Isaiah 42:9*
God declares the end from the beginning—*Isaiah 46:10*
God declares what is to come—*Isaiah 44:7*

Practical Effect on Daily Living
Holiness and godliness—*2 Peter 3:11*
Living without spot or blemish—*2 Peter 3:14*
Personal purity—*1 John 3:3*
Walking properly, avoiding evil—*Romans 13:11-14*

Testifies to God's Greatness
Alpha and Omega—*Revelation 1:8*
Eternal—*Psalms 90:2; 102:12,27; Isaiah 41:13; 57:15; 1 Timothy 1:17; 6:16*
First and the last—*Isaiah 44:6; 48:12*
God's knowledge is infinite—*Psalms 33:13-15; 139:11-12; 147:5; Proverbs 15:3; Isaiah 40:14; 41:22; 46:10; Acts 15:18; Hebrews 4:13; 1 John 3:20*

PROPHETIC POSTPONEMENT
Israel presently hardened—*Matthew 13:13-15; Mark 4:11-12; Luke 8:10; John 12:40; Acts 28:26-27; Romans 11:8-10*
Sixty-ninth and seventieth weeks of Daniel interrupted—*Daniel 9:26-27*
Israel confesses sins and calls to Messiah at end of tribulation (seventieth week)—*Leviticus 26:40-42; Deuteronomy 4:29-31; 30:6-8; Jeremiah 3:11-18; Hosea 5:15; Zechariah 12:10; Romans 9–11*

Prophets

Always accurate—*Deuteronomy 13; 18:20-22*

Called by God—*1 Samuel 3:20; 2 Chronicles 36:15; Jeremiah 1:5; Amos 2:11; Luke 1:13-16*

Called seers—*1 Samuel 9:19; 2 Samuel 15:27; 24:11; 2 Kings 17:13; 1 Chronicles 9:22; 29:29; 2 Chronicles 9:29; 12:15; 29:30; Isaiah 30:10; Micah 3:7*

Controlled by Holy Spirit—*Luke 1:67; Acts 1:16; 11:28; 28:25; 2 Peter 1:21*

Counselors to kings—*Isaiah 37:2-3*

Devout widowed prophetess—*Luke 2:32-36*

Inspired by angels—*Zechariah 1:9,13,14,19; Acts 7:53; Galatians 3:19; Hebrews 2:2*

Intimidating prophetess—*Nehemiah 6:14*

Israel's prophetess and leader—*Judges 4:4-10*

Kept the chronicles—*1 Chronicles 29:29; 2 Chronicles 9:29; 12:15*

Martyrs—*Jeremiah 2:30; Matthew 23:37; Mark 12:5; Luke 13:34; 1 Thessalonians 2:15; Hebrews 11:37; Revelation 16:6*

May hear an audible voice—*Numbers 12:8; 1 Samuel 3:4-14*

Messengers of Lord—*Isaiah 44:26*

Musical prophetess—*Exodus 15:20-21*

Not always honored in their own country—*Matthew 13:57; Luke 4:24-27; John 4:44*

Often endued with miraculous power—*Exodus 4:1-4; 1 Kings 17:23; 2 Kings 5:3-8*

Often spoke words of future deliverance—*Isaiah 6:13; 28:5; 29:5; 31:5*

Often warned people to repent—*Isaiah 1:27; Ezekiel 14:6*

Persecuted—*2 Chronicles 36:16; Amos 2:12*

Predicted Christ's coming—*Luke 24:44; John 1:45; Acts 3:24; 10:43*

Predicted downfall of nations—*Isaiah 15:1; 17:1*

Prophets' accuracy—*1 Samuel 9:6*

Prophetesses (general)—*Exodus 15:20; Judges 4:4; 2 Kings 22:14; Nehemiah 6:14; Isaiah 8:3; Ezekiel 13:17; Joel 2:28-29; Luke 1:41-45; 2:36-38; Acts 21:9; Revelation 2:20*

Receive revelations at various times and in various ways—*Hebrews 1:1*

Receive dreams and visions—*Numbers 12:6; Joel 2:28*

Revelation through prophets—*Exodus 4:11-12,15; Deuteronomy 18:15-22; 1 Samuel 3:19-21; 28:6; 2 Samuel 23:2; 1 Kings 13:20-22; 14:11-12,17; 2 Kings 21:10; 2 Chronicles 20:20; 36:12,16; Isaiah 6:1,8-9; Jeremiah 23:21-22; Ezekiel 1:3; 2:3-5,7; 3:1,10; Hosea 6:5; Joel 2:28-29; Amos 3:7-8; Zechariah 7:7; Acts 3:18; Romans 1:1-2; Hebrews 1:1; 1 Peter 1:10-12; 2 Peter 1:21; Revelation 10:7*

Schools of the prophets—*1 Kings 20:35; 2 Kings 2:3-15; 4:1,38; 9:1*

Secret things revealed—*Amos 3:7*

Sent by Christ—*Matthew 23:34*

Served God and shepherded God's people—*Jeremiah 17:16; Amos 3:7; Zechariah 11:4,7*

Spoke by the Holy Spirit—*Luke 1:67; 2 Peter 1:21*

Spoke in the name of the Lord—*2 Chronicles 33:18; Ezekiel 3:11; James 5:10*

Spoke with authority—*1 Kings 17:1*

Trustworthy prophets—*2 Chronicles 20:20*

PROSTITUTE, GREAT

Prostitution symbolizes unfaithfulness to God—*Jeremiah 3:6-9; Ezekiel 20:30; Hosea 4:15; 5:3; 6:10; 9:1*

Great prostitute symbolizes Babylon, the apostate religious system in the end times that controls nations and people—*Revelation 17:1-2*

Kings of earth commit adultery with this harlot—*Revelation 14:8*

False religious system causes death of saints—*Revelation 17:6*

Will eventually be utterly destroyed—*Revelation 19:2*

PROVIDENCE

In Circumstances

    All things work for good—*Romans 8:28*

    Father cares for us—*Matthew 10:29-31*

    Joseph betrayed by brothers but led to good—*Genesis 45:8; 50:20*

    Length of life—*Job 14:5; Psalm 139:16*

In History

    Controls nations—*Job 12:23-24; Psalm 22:28; Jeremiah 27:5-6; Daniel 4:17*

    Determines when and where people born—*Acts 17:25-27*

    Divine plan—*Acts 4:27-28*

    Sets up kings and deposes them—*Daniel 2:21*

In Nature

    Feeds birds—*Psalm 147:9; Matthew 6:26*

    Provides grass for cattle—*Psalm 104:14*

    Sends rain—*Job 5:10; Psalms 65:9-10; 147:8; Jeremiah 10:13; Acts 14:17*

    See God, *Sovereignty*

PSALMS, BOOK OF

    Fullness of joy in God's presence—*Psalm 16:10-11*

    Eternal life in heaven—*Psalm 23:6*

    God is Israel's defender—*Ezekiel 39*

    God sovereignly rules human history—*Psalms 102:19; 103:19*

    God watches over Israel—*Psalm 121:4*

    God judges people for what they have done—*Psalm 62:12; see also Matthew 16:27*

    Land promises to Abraham—*Psalm 105:8-11*

    Sheol—*Psalms 30:9; 49:15*

    Some messianic psalms are royal psalms—*Psalms 2; 45; 72; 110*

    Some messianic psalms are suffering psalms—*Psalms 16; 22; 40*

PURGATORY

(Problems with this view)
At cross, Jesus said "It is finished"—*John 19:30*
Blood of Jesus purifies from all sin—*1 John 1:7*
Jesus completed the work Father gave Him to do—*John 17:4*
No condemnation for those in Christ Jesus—*Romans 8:1*
Those who believe in Jesus are perfect—*Hebrews 10:14*

PUT (MODERN LIBYA)

In table of nations—*Genesis 10:6*
Nation in end-times coalition that invades Israel—*Ezekiel 38:1-6*
See Ezekiel Invasion; Northern Coalition

R

Rapture

All will be changed—*1 Corinthians 15:50-52*

Awaiting Christ's return—*1 Thessalonians 1:10*

Believers can be confident, unashamed at Lord's coming—*1 John 2:28*

Christ will take the church to the place He prepared in heaven—*John 14:1-3; see also Philippians 3:20; 1 Thessalonians 1:9-10; 3:13; 4:13-18; 5:1-11; 2 Thessalonians 2:1*

Christians will be like Christ—*1 John 3:2-3*

Church delivered from time of trouble—*Revelation 3:10*

Church not appointed to wrath—*1 Thessalonians 1:10; 5:9; see also Romans 5:9*

Church will be raptured—*1 Thessalonians 4:13-17*

Day of the Lord begins at rapture—*1 Thessalonians 5:1-11*

Hope and comfort—*John 14:1-3; 1 Corinthians 15:23-24; 15:51-52; 1 Thessalonians 1:9-10; 2:17-19; 4:13-18; 5:1-11; 2 Thessalonians 2:1-2; James 5:7-9*

Living hope—*1 Peter 1:3-5*

Man of lawlessness revealed after rapture—*2 Thessalonians 2:3*

May the Lord come soon—*1 Corinthians 16:22*

Prepared for rapture—*1 Thessalonians 3:13*

Purified by blessed hope—*Titus 2:11-14*

Rapture is a mystery—*1 Corinthians 15:51-55*

Holy Spirit restrain Antichrist until rapture—*2 Thessalonians 2:7*

Feast of Trumpets may prefigure rapture—*see Leviticus 23:24*

Timothy to be without spot and blame at rapture—*1 Timothy 6:14*

Watch for Lord to come—*Luke 12:35-40*

When trumpet sounds, rapture occurs—*1 Corinthians 15:51-52; 1 Thessalonians 4:16-17*

See Second Coming of Christ; Tribulation Period

Rapture in John and 1 Thessalonians

RAPTURE IN JOHN	RAPTURE IN 1 THESSALONIANS
troubled hearts (John 14:1)	grieve (1 Thessalonians 4:13)
believe in God, believe in Me (John 14:1)	believe Jesus died, believe God will bring (1 Thessalonians 4:14)
I have told you (John 14:2)	we tell you (1 Thessalonians 4:15)
I will come again (John 14:3)	coming of the Lord (1 Thessalonians 4:15)
I will take you to be with Me (John 14:3)	meet the Lord in the air (1 Thessalonians 4:17)
that you also may be where I am (John 14:3)	with the Lord forever (1 Thessalonians 4:17)

Key Components of the Rapture

    Return of Christ—*1 Thessalonians 4:16*

    Resurrection—*1 Thessalonians 4:16*

    Rapture—*1 Thessalonians 4:17*

    Reunion—*1 Thessalonians 4:17*

    Reassurance—*1 Thessalonians 4:18*

    See Pretribulationism

Rapture and Second Coming Are Distinct

RAPTURE	SECOND COMING
Christ comes for His own (John 14:3; 1 Thessalonians 4:17)	Christ comes with His own (Revelation 19:14)
saints return with Christ to heaven (John 14:1-3)	Christ returns to earth (Zechariah 14:4; Acts 1:11)
nations are not judged	nations are judged (Matthew 25:31-46)
imminent (1 Thessalonians 5:1-3)	awaits prophetic signs (Luke 21:11,15)
before day of wrath (1 Thessalonians 1:10; 5:9)	after day of wrath

Rapture—*John 14:1-3; Romans 8:19; 1 Corinthians 1:7-8; 15:51-53; 16:22; Philippians 3:20-21; 4:5; Colossians 3:4; 1 Thessalonians 1:10; 2:19; 4:13-18; 5:9,23; 2 Thessalonians 2:1,3; 1 Timothy 6:14; 2 Timothy 4:1,8; Titus 2:13; Hebrews 9:28; James 5:7-9; 1 Peter 1:7,13; 5:4; 1 John 2:28–3:2; Jude 21; Revelation 2:25; 3:10*

Second coming—*Daniel 2:44-45; 7:9-14; 12:1-3; Zechariah 12:10; 14:1-15; Matthew 13:41; 24:15-31; 26:64; Mark 13:14-27; 14:62; Luke 21:25-28; Acts 1:9-11; 3:19-21; 1 Thessalonians 3:13; 2 Thessalonians 1:6-10; 2:8; 1 Peter 4:12-13; 2 Peter 3:1-14; Jude 14-15; Revelation 1:7; 19:11–20:6; 22:7,12,20*

Readiness

See Second Coming of Christ; Watchfulness

Rebuilding of the Temple

See Temple

Reign of Christ in Millennial Kingdom

Christ full of Holy Spirit—*Isaiah 11:2-3*

Decisive action against any outbreak of sin—*Psalms 2:9; 72:1-4; Isaiah 11:4; 29:20-21; 65:20; 66:24; Jeremiah 31:29-30; Zechariah 14:16-21*

Righteous and just—*Isaiah 3:5-11; 25:2-5; 29:17-21; Micah 5:5-6,10-15; Zechariah 9:3-8*

Unified government—*Ezekiel 37:13-28*

Universal—*Daniel 2:35; 7:14,27; Micah 4:1-2; Zechariah 9:10*

See Millennial Kingdom

Reign with Christ

Believers will reign as a kingdom of priests—*Revelation 5:10*

If we endure, we will reign—*2 Timothy 2:12*

Martyrs will reign—*Revelation 20:4*

Overcomers will sit on throne with Christ—*Revelation 3:21*

Priests of God reign—*Revelation 20:6*

Reign forever—*Revelation 22:5*

Reincarnation

(Problems with this view)

Man dies once, then faces judgment—*Hebrews 9:27*

Christians who die go immediately to heaven—*2 Corinthians 5:8; Philippians 1:21-23*

Unbelievers who die go immediately to place of suffering—*Luke 16:19-31*

People choose their eternal destiny in one lifetime—*Matthew 25:46*

Now is day of salvation—*2 Corinthians 6:2*

Religious System, False (Religious Babylon)

Description of—*Revelation 17:1-7*

Interpretation of—*Revelation 17:8-18*

Controls nations—*Revelation 17:9*

Outwardly glorious, inwardly corrupt—*Revelation 17:4*

Persecutes true believers—*Revelation 17:6*

Powerful political clout—*Revelation 17:12-13*

Unfaithful to truth—*Revelation 17:1,5,15,16*

Worldwide in impact—*Revelation 17:15*

Worship of Antichrist—*1 Timothy 4:1-4; 2 Timothy 3:1-5; 4:1-4; 2 Peter 2:1; 1 John 2:18-19; Jude 4; Revelation 17:1-6*

Violently overthrown—*Revelation 17:16*

Repentance

Makes angels rejoice—*Luke 15:7,10*

Be humble and repent—*2 Chronicles 7:14*

Jesus urges churches to repent—*Revelation 2:5; see also 2:16,21,22; 3:3,19*

Hard-hearted sinners refuse to repent—*Revelation 9:20; 16:9,11*

Confess and find mercy—*Proverbs 28:13*

God commands repentance—*Acts 17:30*

God desires all to repent—*2 Peter 3:9*

Godly sorrow brings repentance—*2 Corinthians 7:10*

God's kindness leads to repentance—*Romans 2:4*
John the Baptist preached repentance—*Matthew 3:1-2*
Produce fruit of repentance—*Matthew 3:8*
Prove repentance by deeds—*Acts 26:20*
Repent and believe good news—*Mark 1:15*
Repent and live—*Ezekiel 18:32*
Repent and turn to God—*Acts 3:19*
Repent, for the kingdom is near—*Matthew 4:17*
Repentance and forgiveness—*Luke 24:47*
Return to God with your whole heart—*Joel 2:12-13*
Unless you repent, you will perish—*Luke 13:3*

RESTORATION OF ALL THINGS

Disciples' question—*Acts 1:6*
Final restoration of all things—*Acts 3:21*
New heaven and new earth—*Revelation 21:1*
See New Heavens and New Earth

RESTRAINER

Holds back Antichrist until He is "out of the way"
—*2 Thessalonians 2:7*
Holy Spirit will be removed from earth with the church at the
rapture—*1 Corinthians 15:50-52; 1 Thessalonians 1:10; 4:13-17; 5:9*
See Holy Spirit

RESURRECTION

Believers will be resurrected—*Job 19:25-27; Psalm 49:15; Isaiah 26:19; John 6:39-40,44,54; 1 Corinthians 6:14; 1 Thessalonians 4:13-17; Revelation 20:4-6*
Dead will hear Christ's voice—*John 5:25,28-29*
We will receive new bodies—*2 Corinthians 5:1-4; Philippians 3:21*
If Christ is not raised, faith is in vain—*1 Corinthians 15:12-21*
Jesus is resurrection and life—*John 11:24-25*

Perishable body becomes imperishable—*1 Corinthians 15:42*
Resurrection of Jesus—*Acts 4:33*
Resurrection of righteous and wicked—*Acts 24:15*
Resurrection will swallow up death—*Isaiah 25:8*
United with Christ in resurrection—*Romans 6:5*
We will all be changed—*1 Corinthians 15:50-52*

Resurrection Appearances of Christ
To ten disciples—*Luke 24:36-43*
To eleven disciples—*John 20:26-29*
To disciples on road to Emmaus—*Luke 24:13-35*
To Mary Magdalene—*John 20:11-17*
To more than 500—*1 Corinthians 15:6*
To Peter—*1 Corinthians 15:5*
To seven disciples at Galilee—*John 21:1-23*
To some women—*Matthew 28:9-10*
To the eleven at the ascension—*Matthew 28:16-20*

Evidences for the Resurrection
First appearance to a woman verifies the account's authenticity—*John 20:1*
Jesus appeared to the disciples—*John 20:19*
Jesus showed the disciples His hands and side—*John 20:20*
Resurrection alone explains apostles' fearless witness—*Acts 5:29-31*
Jesus appeared to Saul (Paul)—*Acts 9*
Jesus appeared to James, who was converted—*John 7:1-5; Acts 1:14; 1 Corinthians 15:7*
Doubting Thomas was convinced—*John 20:24-28*
Jesus gave many convincing proofs over 40 days—*Acts 1:3*
Jesus appeared to more than 500 at same time—*1 Corinthians 15:6*
Early-dated public confession of resurrection—*1 Corinthians 15:1-4*

First Resurrection
> Two types of resurrection: first and second—*Revelation 20:5-6,11-15*
> Of believers—*1 Thessalonians 4:16; Revelation 20:4-5*
> Resurrection of life—*John 5:29*
> Better resurrection—*Hebrews 11:35*

First Resurrection Is Spread Out
> Jesus—*1 Corinthians 15:20,23*
> Church, at the rapture—*1 Thessalonians 4:13-17*
> Two witnesses, during tribulation—*Revelation 11:3,11*
> Tribulation martyrs, at the end of the tribulation—*Revelation 20:4*
> Tribulation converts, at the end of the millennial kingdom—*Revelation 20:5*

Second Resurrection
> Resurrection of unbelievers—*Revelation 20:11-15*
> Last resurrection—*Revelation 20:5; see also verses 6,11-15*
> Resurrection of condemnation—*John 5:29; see also Daniel 12:2; Acts 24:15*

RETURN, CHRIST'S
See Second Coming

REVELATION

General Revelation
> General revelation renders men without excuse—*Romans 1:20*
> Revelation in world of nature—*Psalm 19*

Special Revelation
> God's revelation in history—*Exodus 7–12*
> God's special revelation in Bible—*2 Timothy 3:15-17*
> Promise to John to show him things in heaven—*Revelation 4:1*

Revelation in Jesus Christ—*Matthew 1:23; John 1:14,18; 14:9; Hebrews 1:2-3*

- God's power revealed in Jesus—John 3:2
- God's wisdom revealed in Jesus—1 Corinthians 1:24
- God's love revealed by Jesus—1 John 3:16
- God's grace revealed in Jesus—2 Thessalonians 1:12

Warning against those who would add to prophecy of book of Revelation—*Revelation 22:18-19*

REVELATION, BOOK OF

Description of Jesus in glory—*Revelation 1*
Seven churches of Asia Minor—*Revelation 2–3*
Tribulation—*Revelation 4–18*
Second coming—*Revelation 19*
Millennial kingdom—*Revelation 20*
Eternal state—*Revelation 21–22*
Blessings or beatitudes—*Revelation 1:3; 14:13; 16:15; 19:9; 20:6; 22:7,14*

REWARDS

All believers will stand before judgment seat—*Romans 14:8-10*
Be careful not to lose—*2 John 1:8*
Believers in heaven lay crowns before throne—*Revelation 4:10*
Crown incorruptible—*1 Corinthians 9:25*
Crown of glory—*1 Peter 5:4*
Crown of life—*James 1:12; Revelation 2:10*
Crown of righteousness—*2 Timothy 4:8*
Tree of life—*Revelation 2:7*
Hidden manna and white stone—*Revelation 2:17*
Morning star—*Revelation 2:28*
Inheritance—*Acts 20:32; 26:18; Colossians 1:12; Hebrews 9:15; 1 Peter 1:4; Revelation 21:7*
New name—*Revelation 2:17*

Not harmed by second death—*Revelation 2:11*
Reward is great—*Matthew 5:12; Luke 6:35; Hebrews 10:35*
Robes of righteousness—*Revelation 3:5*
Sit on Christ's throne—*Revelation 3:21*
Some believers may be ashamed—*1 John 2:28*
Some believers may lose rewards—*2 John 8*
Treasure in heaven—*Matthew 19:21; Luke 12:33*

Response to Promise of Rewards
   Diligence—*2 John 1:8*
   Faithfulness—*Revelation 2:10*
   Pressing forward—*Philippians 3:14*
   Rejoicing—*Romans 5:2*
   See Judgment Seat of Christ

RIVER OF LIFE
   Bright as crystal—*Revelation 22:1*
   Flows from throne of God and Lamb—*Revelation 22:1*
   Tree of life on either side of river—*Revelation 22:2*
   Twelve kinds of fruit—*Revelation 22:2*

ROMAN EMPIRE, FUTURE
   Antichrist heads revived Roman empire—*Daniel 2; 7*
   Ten horns: Revived empire, ten nations—*Daniel 7–8*
   Powerful beast: part lion, bear, and leopard—*Daniel 7:7*

ROSH
   From remotest parts of north—*Ezekiel 39:1-2*
   Nation in end-times northern military coalition that invades
      Israel—*Ezekiel 38:2*
   See Ezekiel Invasion; Northern Coalition

SACRIFICES, MILLENNIAL

Millennial temple—*Ezekiel 40–48; see also Isaiah 2:3; 60:13; Joel 3:18*

Temple may symbolize God's presence during millennium—*Ezekiel 37:26-27*

Millennial animal sacrifices—*Isaiah 56:7; 60:7; Jeremiah 33:17-18; Zechariah 14:19-21*

See Animal Sacrifices in the Millennial Temple; Temple

SALVATION

Eternal life promised before the beginning of time—*Titus 1:2*

God sovereign over all our days—*Psalm 139:16*

God's grace given us before beginning of time—*2 Timothy 1:9*

God's plan cannot be thwarted—*Job 42:2*

God's purpose will stand—*Isaiah 46:10*

Kingdom prepared since creation of world—*Matthew 25:34*

Lamb slain from creation of world—*Revelation 13:8*

Lord has purposed, none can thwart—*Isaiah 14:27*

Lord's purpose prevails—*Proverbs 19:21*

Plan slowly revealed—*Colossians 1:26*

Planned in eternity past—*Ephesians 1:1-11*

Timetable for plan—*Galatians 4:4*

Father's Role

Planned and ordained salvation—*John 3:16; Isaiah 53:6,10*

Foreknowledge, predestination, and sovereign calling before time began—*Romans 8:29-30; Ephesians 1:4*

Jesus' Role

Agent of creation—*John 1:3; Colossians 1:16; Hebrews 1:2*

Preincarnate appearances in the Old Testament—*Genesis 16:7; 22:11*

Came to earth as God's ultimate revelation—*John 1:18; Hebrews 1:1-2*
Died on cross as substitutionary sacrifice—*John 3:16*
Resurrected from dead—*1 Peter 1:3; 3:21*
Mediator between Father and humankind—*1 Timothy 2:5*
Second coming—*Revelation 19*

Holy Spirit's Role
Inspired Scripture—*2 Peter 1:21*
Regenerates believers—*Titus 3:5*
Indwells believers—*1 Corinthians 6:19*
Baptizes believers—*1 Corinthians 12:13*
Seals believers—*Ephesians 4:30*
Bestows spiritual gifts—*1 Corinthians 12:11*
See Eternal Life

Sardis
One of seven churches addressed by Christ—*Revelation 3:1-6*
Self-deceived—*Revelation 3:1*
Works incomplete—*Revelation 3:2*
Repent or be disciplined—*Revelation 3:3*
Some true believers—*Revelation 3:4*
Overcomers will be blessed—*Revelation 3:5*

Satan
Accuses and slanders believers—*Job 1:6-11; Revelation 12:10*
Barred from heaven during tribulation—*Revelation 12:9-10*
Deceives whole world—*Revelation 12:9*
Entered into Judas—*Luke 22:3; John 13:27*
Father of lies—*John 8:44*
Fosters spiritual pride—*1 Timothy 3:6*
Gathers armies of world at Armageddon—*Revelation 16:13-16*
God of evil world—*2 Corinthians 4:4*
Has followers—*1 Timothy 5:15*

Hinders answers to prayer—*Daniel 10:12-20*
Instigates jealousy—*James 3:13-16*
Is a cherub—*Ezekiel 28:14*
Jesus came to destroy—*Hebrews 2:14; 1 John 3:8*
Jesus tempted by—*Matthew 4:1-11; Mark 1:13; Luke 4:2*
Leads unholy trinity—*Revelation 13:2; 16:13*
Leads final rebellion against God—*Revelation 20:7-10*
Liar and murderer—*John 8:44*
Lied to Eve—*Genesis 3:4*
Rebelled against God—*Isaiah 14:12-15; Ezekiel 28:13-18*
Masquerades as angel of light—*2 Corinthians 11:14*
One-third of angels followed in rebellion—*Revelation 12:4*
Persecutes Jews in tribulation—*Revelation 12:13-15*
Plants doubt in minds of believers—*Genesis 3:1-5*
Prideful—*1 Timothy 3:6*
Prince of demons—*Matthew 12:24*
Prowls like roaring lion—*1 Peter 5:8*
Resist devil—*James 4:7*
Rose up against Israel—*1 Chronicles 21:1*
Satanic possession—*Mark 3:22*
Spoke to Lord about Job—*Job 1:6-9,12*
Synagogue of Satan—*Revelation 2:9*
Tempts believers to immorality—*1 Corinthians 7:5*
Tempts believers to lie—*Acts 5:3*
Wear spiritual armor for protection—*Ephesians 6:11-18*
Will be bound in chains for thousand years—*Revelation 20:2*
Worked through Peter—*Matthew 16:23*
See Demons

Names and Descriptions
Accuser of brethren—*Revelation 12:10*
Beelzebub—*Matthew 12:24*
Belial—*2 Corinthians 6:15*

Devil—*1 Peter 5:8*
Dragon—*Revelation 12:3*
Evil one—*1 John 5:19*
God of this age—*2 Corinthians 4:4*
Lucifer—*Isaiah 14:12*
Prince of the power of the air—*Ephesians 2:2*
Prince of this world—*John 12:31*
Satan—*2 Corinthians 11:14*
Serpent—*Revelation 12:9*
Tempter—*1 Thessalonians 3:5*

Scoffers

Unbelief and scoffing will predominate in end times—*2 Peter 3:3*
"Where is the promise of his coming?"—*2 Peter 3:4*
In last time, scoffers will follow ungodly passions—*Jude 18*
See also 2 Chronicles 30:6-10; 36:16; Job 21:14-15; 34:7;
    Psalms 1:1; 42:3; 73:11; 78:19-20; 107:11-12; Proverbs
    1:22,25; 3:34; 9:12; 13:1; 14:6,9; 19:29; 21:11,24; 22:10;
    24:9; Isaiah 5:18-19,24-25; 10:15; 29:20; 57:4; Jeremiah
    17:15; 43:2; Lamentations 1:7; Ezekiel 8:12; 9:9; 11:2-3;
    12:22; 33:20; Hosea 7:5

Scripture

Inerrancy

All God's words are true—*Psalm 119:160*
Every jot and tittle is accurate—*Matthew 5:17-18*
Every word of God is flawless—*Psalms 12:6; 18:30; Proverbs
    30:5-6*
God's commands are true—*Psalm 119:151*
God's word is truth—*John 17:17*
Law of Lord is perfect—*Psalm 19:7*
Ordinances of Lord are sure—*Psalm 19:9*
Scripture cannot be broken—*John 10:35*

Singular word is accurate—*Galatians 3:16*
Words from God—*Matthew 4:4*

Inspiration

All Scripture is inspired—*2 Timothy 3:16*
Christ spoke through Paul—*2 Corinthians 13:2-3*
God inscribed two stone tablets—*Exodus 31:18*
God put His words in Jeremiah's mouth—*Jeremiah 1:9; 5:14*
God taught Moses what to speak—*Exodus 4:12-16*
Holy Spirit guided apostles into truth—*John 14:26; 16:13*
Holy Spirit moved biblical writers—*2 Peter 1:21*
Holy Spirit spoke through David—*2 Samuel 23:2-3; Acts 1:16; 4:25*
Jeremiah wrote God's words—*Jeremiah 30:1-2*
Luke's Gospel is Scripture—*1 Timothy 5:18*
Paul wrote at Lord's command—*1 Corinthians 14:37*
Paul's words were God's words—*1 Thessalonians 2:13*
Paul's writings are Scripture—*2 Peter 3:16*
Scripture cannot be broken—*John 10:35*
Words of Scripture taught by Holy Spirit—*1 Corinthians 2:13*

SEA OF GLASS

Before God's throne—*Revelation 4:6*
Under God's feet is pavement made of sapphire, clear as sky—*Exodus 24:10*

SEAL JUDGMENTS

First seal: White horse, rider went out to conquer—*Revelation 6:1-2*
Second seal: No peace, swords slay one another—*Revelation 6:3-4*
Third seal: Widespread famine—*Revelation 6:5-6*
Fourth seal: Massive death by famine, pestilence, wild beasts—*Revelation 6:7-8*
Fifth seal: Martyrs and more martyrs—*Revelation 6:9-11*

Sixth seal: Earthquake, cosmic disturbances, people hiding—*Revelation 6:12-17*

Seventh seal: Trumpet judgments—*Revelation 8*

SECOND ADVENT

See Second Coming of Christ

SECOND COMING OF CHRIST

Anticipated—*Psalm 110:1; Isaiah 2:2-4; 42:4; Daniel 7:13-14; Joel 2:30-32; Zechariah 14:3-4; Malachi 3:1; Hebrews 9:28*

Appearing of great God and Savior Jesus Christ—*Titus 2:11-14*

As Judge—*Psalm 50:3-4; John 5:22; 2 Timothy 4:1; Jude 15; Revelation 20:11-13*

Christ is Alpha and Omega who is to come—*Revelation 1:8*

Climax of the ages—*Ephesians 1:10*

Coming as Lord and King—*Hebrews 9:24-28*

Coming from heaven—*1 Thessalonians 1:10*

Coming in clouds—*Matthew 24:30; 26:64; Revelation 1:7*

Coming soon—*Philippians 4:5; Hebrews 10:37; James 5:7-8; Revelation 3:11; 22:12,20*

Coming visibly—*Acts 1:9-11*

Completes salvation of believers—*Hebrews 9:28; 1 Peter 1:5*

Crown of righteousness for those longing for His coming—*2 Timothy 4:8*

Day of His coming—*Malachi 3:2*

Desire of all nations will come—*Haggai 2:7*

Every eye will see Him—*Zechariah 12:10; Revelation 1:7*

Israel will welcome her coming King—*Zechariah 9:9-17*

Judgment of the nations follows—*Matthew 25:31-46*

Last days conduct—*2 Timothy 3:1-5*

Messiah of Israel will come in triumph—*Zechariah 14:1-8*

Mistaken information as to return—*John 21:20-23*

No one knows hour—*Matthew 24:42,44,46-50; Mark 13:32-37; Luke 21:34-36*

Prepared for second coming—*1 Thessalonians 3:13*
Promise of Christ's coming, reaffirmed—*Revelation 22:12*
Rapture—*1 Thessalonians 4:13-17*
Remnant of Israel rescued at Christ's return—*Isaiah 64:1-12*
Return of Lord Jesus—*1 Corinthians 1:7-8; Hebrews 9:28*
Scoffers in last days—*2 Peter 3:4*
Signs in sun, moon, stars—*Luke 21:25,27*
Those not ready punished—*Matthew 24:45-51*
Vision of Christ's coming—*Daniel 7:9-14*
Watch for Lord to come—*Luke 12:35-40*
We eagerly wait—*Philippians 3:20; Titus 2:13*
We will be like Him—*1 John 3:2*
Will come back on clouds of heaven—*Matthew 26:64*
Will come in glory—*Matthew 16:27; 25:31; Mark 8:38; Luke 9:26*
Worldwide spectacle—*Matthew 24:30*
Yearning for Messiah—*Isaiah 64:1*

Accompanying the Second Coming
Angels—*Matthew 16:27; 25:31; Mark 8:38; 2 Thessalonians 1:7*
Armies of heaven—*Revelation 19:11,14*
Blazing fire—*2 Thessalonians 1:7*
Clouds of heaven—*Daniel 7:13; Matthew 24:30; 26:64; Acts 1:9-11; Revelation 1:7*
Cosmic phenomena—*Matthew 24:29; Mark 13:24-25; Luke 21:25-26; Acts 2:19-20; 2 Peter 3:10; Revelation 6:12-14*
Church—*Colossians 3:4; Jude 14; Revelation 19:14*
Gathering of saints to Jesus—*Matthew 24:31; Mark 13:27; 1 Corinthians 15:50-57; 1 Thessalonians 4:16-17; Revelation 19:6-9*
Multitude of holy followers—*1 Thessalonians 3:13; Jude 14*

Characteristics of Jesus' Second Coming
Glorious—*Matthew 16:27; 24:30; 25:31; Titus 2:13*
Holy and just—*Revelation 19:11-13,15-16*

Personal—*Mark 8:38; John 21:20-22; Acts 1:10-11; 1 Corinthians 4:5; 1 Thessalonians 2:19-20*
Powerful—*Matthew 24:30; 2 Peter 3:10*
Visible—*Zechariah 12:10; Mark 13:26; Acts 1:11; Revelation 1:7*

Predictions of Second Coming
Angels—*Acts 1:10-11*
Apostles—*Acts 3:20; 1 Timothy 6:14*
Christ—*Matthew 25:31; John 14:3*
Prophets—*Daniel 7:13; Jude 14*

Significance for People
Gather His followers—*1 Thessalonians 4:17; 2 Thessalonians 2:1*
Raise the dead—*John 5:28-29; 1 Corinthians 15:22-23; 1 Thessalonians 4:16*
Reward believers—*Matthew 16:27; 24:46-47; 1 Thessalonians 2:19; 2 Timothy 4:8; 1 Peter 5:4; Revelation 22:12*
Separate wicked from righteous—*Matthew 24:40-41; 25:31-32*
Transform bodies of believers—*1 Corinthians 15:51-53; Philippians 3:20-21*

Sudden and Unexpected
As lightning—*Matthew 24:27*
As Noah's flood—*Matthew 24:37-41; Luke 17:26-27,30*
As the coming of the bridegroom—*Matthew 25:1-13*
As the destruction of Sodom—*Luke 17:28-30*
As thief in night—*Matthew 24:42-44; 1 Thessalonians 5:2-3; 2 Peter 3:10; Revelation 16:15*
At the final consummation of history—*1 Corinthians 1:8; 1 Peter 1:5*
Soon—*Philippians 4:5; Hebrews 10:37; James 5:8-9; Revelation 22:7,20*
Like a thief—*1 Thessalonians 5:1-3; Revelation 16:15*
Sudden—*Mark 13:33-36; 1 Thessalonians 5:2-3*
Time known only by God—*Matthew 24:36-41; Acts 1:6-7; 1 Timothy 6:14-15*

No one knows the hour—*Matthew 24:36,42,44,46-50; 24:36; Mark 13:32; Luke 12:35-40*

Attitudes While We Wait
Await Master—*Luke 12:36*
Be blameless until He comes—*1 Thessalonians 5:23; 1 Timothy 6:13-15*
Be faithful until He returns—*1 Timothy 6:11-16*
Be on alert; don't know when Master is coming—*Mark 13:35*
Be patient awaiting Lord's return—*James 5:7*
Be ready for bridegroom—*Matthew 25:10*
Bride made ready—*Revelation 19:7*
Readiness—*Luke 12:35*
Soberness—*1 Thessalonians 5:6; 1 Timothy 3:2,11; Titus 1:8; 2:2,12; 1 Peter 1:13; 4:7*
See Eternal Perspective; Watchfulness; Millennial Kingdom; Rapture; Tribulation Period

Second Death
Eternal separation from God in lake of fire—*Revelation 20:14*
Follows Great White Throne judgment—*Revelation 20:11-15*
See Death

Second Resurrection
Resurrection of unbelievers—*Revelation 20:11-15*
Resurrection of condemnation—*John 5:29; see also Daniel 12:2; Acts 24:15*
Last resurrection—*Revelation 20:5; see also verses 6,11-15*
See Resurrection

Selfishness
Last days, lovers of selves—*2 Timothy 3:2; see also 1 Corinthians 10:24; 2 Corinthians 5:15; Galatians 6:2; Philippians 2:4*

SENSATIONALISM
Be of sound judgment and sober spirit—*1 Peter 4:7*
Be sober—*1 Thessalonians 5:6*
Live soberly—*Titus 2:1*
See Eternal Perspective; Watchfulness

SEVEN CHURCHES OF REVELATION
Ephesus—*Revelation 2:1-7*
Smyrna—*Revelation 2:8-11*
Pergamum—*Revelation 2:12-17*
Thyatira—*Revelation 2:18-29*
Sardis—*Revelation 3:1-6*
Philadelphia—*Revelation 3:7-13*
Laodicea—*Revelation 3:14-22*

SEVEN MOUNTAINS
Seven kingdoms—*Revelation 17:9-10; see also Psalm 30:7; Jeremiah 51:25; Daniel 2:44-45*

SEVEN SPIRITS OF GOD
Before throne of God—*Revelation 1:4*
Jesus has the seven spirits of God—*Revelation 3:1*
Before throne, seven torches, seven spirits of God—*Revelation 4:5*
Lamb has "seven eyes, which are the seven spirits of God"—*Revelation 5:6*
Seven-fold ministry of Holy Spirit—*Isaiah 11:2*
See Holy Spirit

SEVENTY WEEKS OF DANIEL
From end of exile to Christ's advent: 69 weeks (of years)—*Daniel 9:25*
A gap then occurs—*Daniel 9:26*
Antichrist's covenant begins the tribulation, the seventieth week (of years)—*Daniel 9:27*
See Tribulation Period

Sheep and Goats

Sheep are God's people, they enter God's kingdom—*Matthew 25:33-40*

Goats are unbelievers; they are eternally punished—*Matthew 25:41-46*

Sheol

In Old Testament times, believed to be destiny of righteous and unrighteous—*Genesis 37:35; Psalm 9:17; Isaiah 38:10*

Full of horror—*Psalm 30:9*

Grave—*Psalm 49:15*

Place of punishment—*Job 24:19*

Place of weeping—*Isaiah 38:3*

Shadowy and gloomy—*2 Samuel 22:6; Ecclesiastes 9:10*

Underground region—*Numbers 16:30,33; Amos 9:2*

Signs of the Times

Apostasy—*Matthew 24:3,10; 2 Timothy 4:3-4*

Appearance of Antichrist—*Matthew 24:5,23-24,26; Luke 21:8; 2 Thessalonians 2:1-10; 1 John 2:18-23; 4:3; 2 John 7; Revelation 13:1-8; 19:20*

Betrayal—*Mark 13:3-4,12; Luke 21:16*

Departure from the faith—*1 Timothy 4:1*

Earthquakes—*Matthew 24:7; Mark 13:8*

False Christs—*Matthew 24:24-25; Mark 13:5,21-23; Luke 21:8; John 5:41-44*

False prophets—*Matthew 24:11; Mark 13:6,21-23*

False signs and miracles—*Matthew 24:24; Mark 13:22; Luke 21:8; 2 Thessalonians 2:9-10; Revelation 19:20*

Famines—*Matthew 24:7; Mark 13:8; Revelation 6:5-6*

General time (parable of fig tree)—*Matthew 24:33*

Increase of evil—*Matthew 24:12; 2 Timothy 3:1-5; 2 Peter 3:3-4*

Innumerable vices—*2 Timothy 3:1-5*

International strife—*Matthew 24:7; Mark 13:8; Luke 21:10; Revelation 6:3-4*

Lawlessness—*Matthew 24:12*

Many fall away—*Matthew 24:10*

Persecution of believers—*Matthew 24:8-9; Mark 13:9-11,13; Luke 21:12-17; 2 Timothy 3:1-5,10-13; Revelation 6:9-11; 12:17; 20:4*

Pestilence—*Luke 21:11; Revelation 6:7-8*

Tribulation, death, hatred of believers—*Matthew 24:9*

Unparalleled distress—*Matthew 24:21; Mark 13:17-19; Luke 21:23*

Wars, rumors of wars—*Matthew 24:6; Mark 13:7; Luke 21:9*

Worldwide proclamation of gospel—*Matthew 24:14; Mark 13:10; Revelation 14:6-7*

SLEEP (DEATH)

Jesus, the firstfruits of those who have fallen asleep—*1 Corinthians 15:20*

Lazarus asleep—*John 11:11*

Many have fallen asleep—*1 Thessalonians 4:15*

Some in Corinth fell asleep in judgment—*1 Corinthians 11:30*

Stephen fell asleep—*Acts 7:60*

We shall not all sleep—*1 Corinthians 15:51*

See Death

SMYRNA

One of seven churches in Asia Minor Christ addressed—*Revelation 2:8-11*

Poverty of—*Revelation 2:9*

Tested—*Revelation 2:10*

Devil persecutes—*Revelation 2:10*

Exhorted to be faithful, receive crown of life—*Revelation 2:10*

Overcomers receive blessings—*Revelation 2:11*

SON OF MAN

"Son of Man" a messianic term—*Daniel 7:13*

Jesus called Himself—*Matthew 8:20; 20:18; 24:30*
Jesus fully God—*Matthew 16:16-17; John 8:58; 10:30*
Jesus fully man—*Philippians 2:6-8*
Son of Man forgives sins (and is therefore God)—*Isaiah 43:25; Mark 2:7,10*
Jesus coming again as Son of Man—*Matthew 26:63-64*
See Jesus Christ, *Names and Titles*

Sign of the Son of Man
Sign will appear at second coming—*Matthew 24:29-30*
Some suggest it is lightning from east to west—*Matthew 24:27*
Some suggest it is Son of Man Himself—*see Daniel 7:13; Acts 1:11; Revelation 19:11-21*

SORCERIES

Worshipping demons, idolatry, and sorcery in tribulation—*Revelation 9:20-21*
Magic arts in tribulation—*Revelation 21:8; 22:15*
Diviners will be disgraced—*Micah 3:7*
Egyptian magicians, secret arts—*Exodus 7:11,22; 8:7,18*
Magicians, enchanters, sorcerers—*Daniel 2:2*
Fortune-telling and sorcery forbidden—*Deuteronomy 18:10-11*
No more fortune-tellers—*Micah 5:12*
Sorcery and divination—*2 Kings 21:6*
Using cups for divination—*Genesis 44:2,5*
Wizards—*1 Samuel 28:3*
See Occultism

STARS

Sun becomes black, moon like blood during tribulation—*Revelation 6:12*
Sun darkened, moon darkened, stars fall, heavens shake at second coming—*Matthew 24:29-30*

Third of light of sun, moon, stars darkened during tribulation—
Revelation 8:12

See also Isaiah 13:10; 24:23; Ezekiel 32:7; Joel 2:10,31; 3:15;
Amos 5:20; 8:9; Zephaniah 1:15; Acts 2:20

Sun

See Stars

Temple

Tribulation temple

Antichrist will exalt himself as God in the tribulation temple—
2 Thessalonians 2:4

Temple must be rebuilt for abomination of desolation to
occur—*Matthew 24:15-16*

See Daniel 9:27; 12:11

Millennium temple

Jerusalem will have temple in millennial kingdom—*Ezekiel
40–48; see also Isaiah 2:3; 60:13; Joel 3:18*

Temple built at beginning of kingdom—*Ezekiel 37:26-28*

Built by Christ, redeemed Jews, and representatives from
Gentile nations—*Ezekiel 43:10-11; Haggai 2:7; Zechariah
6:12-13,15*

Symbol of God's presence—*Ezekiel 37:26-27*

Redeemed Gentiles included in worship in millennial temple—
Isaiah 60:6; Zephaniah 3:10; Zechariah 2:11

Jesus will be worshipped—*Jeremiah 33:15-22; Ezekiel 40–48;
Zechariah 14:16-21*

Millennial animal sacrifices—*Isaiah 56:7; 60:7; Jeremiah 33:17-
18; Zechariah 14:19-21*

Ten-Horned Beast

Revived Roman empire, ten nations—*Daniel 7–8*

Antichrist ("little horn") heads revived Roman empire—*Daniel
2; 7–8*

Roman empire a terrifying and powerful mongrel beast—*Daniel
7:7*

See Antichrist

Test the Spirits

Test the spirits—*1 John 4:1*
Be like Bereans—*Acts 17:11*
Test all things—*1 Thessalonians 5:21*
Word of God is the barometer of truth—*2 Timothy 3:15-17*
See Bible

Thessalonians, 1 and 2

Antichrist emerges prior to second coming—*2 Thessalonians 2:1-12*
Antichrist glorifies himself—*2 Thessalonians 2:4*
Antichrist's blasphemous nature—*2 Thessalonians 2:3-11*
Antichrist's counterfeit signs and wonders—*2 Thessalonians 2:9-10*
Rapture—*1 Thessalonians 4:13-17; 5:1-3*
Be blameless until Christ comes—*1 Thessalonians 5:23*
Be joyful always—*1 Thessalonians 5:16*
Calamity in 1 Thessalonians 5:1-3 is post-rapture event—*see 1 Thessalonians 4:13-17*
Call of archangel—*1 Thessalonians 4:16*
Christ will come like thief—*1 Thessalonians 5:1-3*
Church not appointed to wrath—*1 Thessalonians 1:10; 5:9*
Dead in Christ will rise—*1 Thessalonians 4:13-17*
Continue working—*2 Thessalonians 3:6-13*
Destruction will fall when people claim peace and safety—*1 Thessalonians 5:1-3*
End-times apostasy—*2 Thessalonians 2:3*
Hope gives endurance—*1 Thessalonians 1:3*
Man of lawlessness—*2 Thessalonians 2:1-10*
Prophecy encourages—*1 Thessalonians 4:18*
Restrainer hinders emergence of Antichrist until "out of the way"—*2 Thessalonians 2:7*
Temple rebuilt during tribulation—*2 Thessalonians 2:4*
We await God's Son—*1 Thessalonians 1:10*
We will always be with Lord—*1 Thessalonians 4:17*

THRONE OF DAVID

Descendant of David will rule forever—*2 Samuel 7:12-13; 22:51;
1 Chronicles 17:10-14*

Fulfilled in Jesus, born from line of David—*Matthew 1:1; Luke
1:32-33*

Jesus will rule on throne of David in Jerusalem during
millennial kingdom—*Isaiah 2:1-4; 9:6-7; 11:1-10; 16:5;
24:23; 32:1-2; 40:1-11; 42:3-4; 52:7-15; Jeremiah 23:5-6;
33:17-26; Ezekiel 36:1-12; Daniel 2:44; 7:27; Amos 9:11-12;
Micah 4:1-5; 5:2-5; Zephaniah 3:14-20; Zechariah 9:9; 14:1-21*

See Davidic Covenant

THRONE OF GOD

Lord has established throne in heaven—*Psalm 103:19*

Lord is on heavenly throne—*Psalm 11:4*

For judgment—*Psalm 9:7*

From all eternity—*Psalm 93:2*

Majestic and awesome—*Revelation 4:2-6*

Lasts forever—*Psalm 45:6*

Believers before God's throne day and night—*Revelation 7:15*

THYATIRA

One of seven churches in Asia Minor addressed by Christ—
Revelation 2:18-28

Commended for love, faith, service, endurance—*Revelation 2:19*

Chastised for tolerating Jezebel—*Revelation 2:21*

Judgment promised unless repentance—*Revelation 2:22-23*

TIME

An appointed season—*Nehemiah 2:6; Ecclesiastes 3:1,17*

Christ created "the ages"—*Hebrews 1:2*

Day is like thousand years to Lord—*2 Peter 3:8*

Days—*Genesis 8:3; Job 1:4; Luke 11:3*

God set boundaries for day and night—*Job 26:10*

In beginning God created—*Genesis 1:1*

Moments of time—*Exodus 33:5; Luke 4:5; 1 Corinthians 15:52*
Months—*Numbers 10:10; 1 Chronicles 27:1; Job 3:6*
Shortness of time for man—*Psalm 89:47*
Signs to mark seasons—*Genesis 1:14*
Time of healing—*Jeremiah 14:19*
Time of need—*Hebrews 4:16*
Time of reformation—*Hebrews 9:10*
Time of refreshing—*Acts 3:19*
Time of restoration—*Acts 3:21*
Time of temptation—*Luke 8:13*
Time should be redeemed—*Ephesians 5:16; Colossians 4:5*
Time should be spent in fear of God—*1 Peter 1:17*
Weeks—*Daniel 10:2; Luke 18:12*
Fullness of time—*Galatians 4:4*
Years—*Genesis 15:13; 2 Samuel 21:1; Daniel 9:2*
See Eternity

Time of Jacob's Trouble

Tribulation called "time of Jacob's trouble"—*Jeremiah 30:7*
Details of distress—*Revelation 6–18*
See Tribulation Period

Times of the Gentiles

Time of Gentile domination on Jerusalem—*Luke 21:24*
Will last into the tribulation—*Revelation 11:2*

Transfiguration

Jesus transfigured before disciples—*Matthew 17:2*
Appearance of face changed—*Luke 9:29*
Face shone like sun—*Matthew 17:2*
Clothing white as light—*Matthew 17:2*
Clothing dazzling white—*Mark 9:3*
Preview of Christ's glory at second coming—*Acts 15:14-18;
   1 Corinthians 15:20-28; Revelation 1:14-15; 19:15; 20:4-6*

TREE OF LIFE

First seen in Garden of Eden—*Genesis 2:9,17; 3:1-24*
Cherubim guards—*Genesis 3:24*
In paradise of God—*Revelation 2:7*
On either side of river of life—*Revelation 22:2*
Twelve kinds of fruit—*Revelation 22:2*
Leaves bring healing to nations—*Revelation 22:2*

TRIBULATION GOVERNMENT

World government dominated by Satan and beast—*Revelation 13:1-2*
Leader of world empire, fatal wound—*Revelation 13:3*
Beast exercises authority 42 months—*Revelation 13:5-6*
Beast described as political power of end time—*Revelation 17:9-13*
Babylon will fall and be destroyed at end of tribulation—*Revelation 14:8; 18*
Fate of world governments—*Psalm 2:7-9*

TRIBULATION PERIOD

Cosmic disturbances—*Luke 21:25-26; Revelation 8:12. See also Isaiah 13:10; 24:23; Ezekiel 32:7; Joel 2:10,31; 3:15; Amos 5:20; 8:9; Zephaniah 1:15; Matthew 24:29-30; Acts 2:20; Revelation 6:12*
Angels bound at Euphrates are released during tribulation—*Revelation 9:14*
Antichrist will demand worship—*2 Thessalonians 2:4*
Babylon is headquarters of Antichrist during tribulation—*Revelation 17–18*
Darkness—*Amos 5:18*
Day of alarm—*Zephaniah 1:16*
Day of calamity—*Deuteronomy 32:35; Obadiah 12–14*
Day of gloom—*Joel 2:2; Amos 5:18,20; Zephaniah 1:15*
Day of Lord's anger—*Zephaniah 2:2-3*
Day of ruin—*Joel 1:15*
Day of thick darkness—*Joel 2:2; Zephaniah 1:15*

Day of vengeance—*Isaiah 34:8; 35:4; 61:2; 63:4*
Day of waste—*Zephaniah 1:15*
Demons torment those on earth—*Revelation 9:3*
Desolation—*Daniel 9:27*
Destruction—*Joel 1:15*
Devil barred from heaven during—*Revelation 12:9-10*
Dominion of Antichrist—*Revelation 13*
Events of tribulation—*Revelation 4–18*
Final "week" of seven years, Antichrist signs covenant—*Daniel 9:27*
Great and terrible day—*Malachi 4:5*
Great tribulation—*Matthew 24:21*
Hour of judgment—*Revelation 14:7*
Hour of trial—*Revelation 3:10*
Imminent rapture prior to—*1 Thessalonians 4:13-17*
Indignation—*Isaiah 26:20-21*
Israel's conversion at end of tribulation—*Romans 9–11*
Judgments of tribulation—*Isaiah 24:1-23; Revelation 14:7*
No New Testament passage on tribulation mentions church—
     Matthew 13:30,39-42,48-50; 24:15-31; 1 Thessalonians 1:9-10;
     5:4-9; 2 Thessalonians 2:1-11; Revelation 4–18
No Old Testament passage on tribulation mentions church—
     Deuteronomy 4:29-30; Jeremiah 30:4-11; Daniel 8:24-27; 12:1-2
Overturning—*Isaiah 24:1-4*
People will faint with fear—*Luke 21:25-26*
People will long for death—*Revelation 9:6*
Punishment—*Isaiah 24:20-21*
Scourge—*Isaiah 28:15,18*
Second coming ends tribulation—*Micah 2:12-13*
Seven years long—*Daniel 9:27*
Sun becomes black, full moon like blood—*Revelation 6:12*
Temple rebuilt during tribulation—*2 Thessalonians 2:4*
Time of distress—*Daniel 12:1*
Time of Jacob's distress—*Jeremiah 30:7*

Trial—*Revelation 3:10*
Trouble—*Jeremiah 30:7*
Worldwide—*Revelation 3:10*
Wrath—*Zephaniah 1:15,18*
Wrath of Lamb—*Revelation 6:16-17*
Wrath of God—*Revelation 14:10,19; 15:1,7; 16:1*
Wrath to come—*1 Thessalonians 1:10*
Year of recompense—*Isaiah 34:8*
See Antichrist; Millennial Kingdom; Rapture; Second Coming of Christ

TRIBULATION AND THE BEGINNING OF SORROWS

Includes rise of false Christs, wars, nations embattled, famines, earthquakes—*Matthew 24:1-7*
Olivet Discourse, "beginning of sorrows"—*Matthew 24:8*
Parallel to seal judgments—*see Revelation 6:1-14*
See Tribulation Period

TRIBULATION MARTYRDOM

Antipas—*Revelation 2:13*
Be faithful unto death—*Revelation 2:10*
Beast wars against saints—*Revelation 13:7*
Believers who die in tribulation are blessed—*Revelation 14:13*
Great multitude martyred—*Revelation 7:9-10*
Martyred dead of tribulation are raised to reign with Christ—*Revelation 20:4-6*
Tribulation martyrs given white robes—*Revelation 6:11*
Tribulation martyrs seek vengeance for deaths—*Revelation 6:10*
Tribulation martyrs told more martyrs to follow—*Revelation 6:11*
Tribulation martyrs under God's altar—*Revelation 6:9*
Two witnesses martyred—*Revelation 11:7*

TRIBULATION SAINTS

Saints in church raptured before tribulation—*1 Thessalonians 1:10; 4:13-17; 5:9; Revelation 3:10*

Many conversions during tribulation—*see Matthew 25:31-46; Revelation 7:9-10*

Conversions due to 144,000 Jewish evangelists—*Revelation 7:14*

Conversions due to two witnesses—*Revelation 11*

TRUMPET JUDGMENTS

First trumpet judgment: hail, fire, earth burned—*Revelation 8:7*

Second trumpet judgment: fiery mountain into sea, sea turns bloody, third of sea creatures die—*Revelation 8:8*

Third trumpet judgment: star falls from heaven, poisons water—*Revelation 8:10-11*

Fourth trumpet judgment: severe cosmic disturbances—*Revelation 8:12-13*

Fifth trumpet judgment: demons released from bottomless pit, torment men—*Revelation 9:1-12*

Sixth trumpet judgment: angels bound at Euphrates released, kill a third of mankind—*Revelation 9:13-21*

Seventh trumpet judgment: bowl judgments—*see Revelation 16*

TUBAL

In table of nations—*Genesis 10:2*

Nation in northern military coalition that will invade Israel in end times—*Ezekiel 38:1-6; see also Ezekiel 27:13; 32:26; 39:1*

See Ezekiel Invasion; Northern Coalition

TWENTY-FOUR ELDERS

Cast their crowns before the Lord—*Revelation 4:4,10-11*

Fall down before the Lord—*Revelation 5:8; 19:4*

Sit on thrones and worship—*Revelation 11:16*

TWINKLING OF AN EYE

Rapture occurs in twinkling of eye—*1 Corinthians 15:51-52; see also John 14:1-3; 1 Thessalonians 1:10; 4:13-17; 5:9; Titus 2:13; Revelation 3:10*

See Rapture

Two Witnesses

Prophesy 1260 days—*Revelation 11:3*

Fire consumes those who try to kill—*Revelation 11:5*

Miraculous powers—*Revelation 11:6*

Put to death—*Revelation 11:7*

Dead bodies lie in street—*Revelation 11:8*

People make merry at their death—*Revelation 11:9-10*

Resurrect from dead—*Revelation 11:11*

Ascend to heaven—*Revelation 11:12*

Similar to Elijah—*1 Kings 17; Malachi 4:5*

Similar to Moses—*Exodus 7–11*

See Prophets

Typology (Illustrated in Joseph)

Both Joseph and Christ were born by special intervention of God—*Genesis 30:22-24; Luke 1:35*

Both were objects of special love by fathers—*Genesis 37:3; Matthew 3:17; John 3:35*

Both were hated by brethren—*Genesis 37:4; John 15:24-25*

Both were robbed of robes—*Genesis 37:23; Matthew 27:35*

Both were conspired against—*Genesis 37:18,24; Matthew 26:3-4; 27:35-37*

Both were sold for silver—*Genesis 37:28; Matthew 26:14-15*

Both were condemned though innocent—*Genesis 39:11-20; Isaiah 53:9; Matthew 27:19,24*

Both were raised from humiliation to glory—*Genesis 45:16-18; Isaiah 65:17-25*

UNITED STATES IN PROPHECY
See America in Biblical Prophecy

UNIVERSALISM
(Problems with this view)
Faith in Savior required—*John 3:16,18,36; 5:24; Acts 16:30-31; Roman 3:21; 4:5; James 2:23*
Two classes of people in end (saved and unsaved)—*Matthew 13:30,49; 25:32,34,46*
Two destinies in the end:

- Heaven—Matthew 10:22,37-39; 18:8-9; 19:16-29; 24:34-40,46; John 12:26,47-48,50; Acts 11:18; Romans 2:7; 6:22; 8:11; Galatians 6:8; 1 Timothy 4:8; 2 Timothy 2:10-12; James 1:12; Revelation 2:7,11,17; 3:5,12,21; 14:4-5; 21:2,7; 22:14

- Hell—Matthew 7:19,21-23; 13:38,40-41; 23:29-33; 25:41; Luke 8:11-12; John 3:18,36; 1 Corinthians 1:18,21-23; 6:9-10; Galatians 5:19-21; Ephesians 5:5; 2 Thessalonians 2:8-12; Hebrews 3:12-19; 4:1-3; 6:4,6,8; 1 John 5:12; Jude 5; Revelation 19:19-20; 20:10,13-14; 21:8; 22:14-15

UNTHANKFUL
Last days, lovers of selves, ungrateful, unthankful—*2 Timothy 3:2; see also 1 Corinthians 10:24; 2 Corinthians 5:15; Galatians 6:2; Philippians 2:4*

VALLEY OF DRY BONES

Israel to be rebuilt—*Ezekiel 36:10*
Gathered from many nations—*Ezekiel 36:24*
Israel again to be prosperous—*Ezekiel 36:30*
Bones come back together—*Ezekiel 37:7*
Sinews, flesh, and skin grow over bones—*Ezekiel 37:8*
Breath given to body—*Ezekiel 37:9-10*
Bones coming together are whole house of Israel—*Ezekiel 37:11*
See Israel, *Rebirth of*

VISION

Revelation from God—*Numbers 12:6; Hebrews 1:1; Luke 24:23; Acts 26:19; 2 Corinthians 12:1*
Some visions relate to seeing God—*Isaiah 6:1-5*
Some visions relate to heavenly realities—*Book of Revelation*
Some visions relate to earthly realities—*1 Kings 22:15-17*
End-times vision: Ezekiel and dry bones, Israel becomes nation again—*Ezekiel 37*
Audible voice—*Genesis 15:1; 1 Samuel 3:4-5*
Difficult and perplexing—*Daniel 7:15; 8:15; Acts 10:17*
Trance—*Numbers 24:16; Acts 11:5*
Prophets of God skilled in interpreting—*2 Chronicles 26:5; Daniel 1:17*
False prophets pretend to have seen—*Jeremiah 14:14; 23:16*
See Revelation

Daniel's Visions

Four beasts—*Daniel 7*
Ancient of Days—*Daniel 7:9-27*
Ram and the he-goat—*Daniel 8*
Angel—*Daniel 10*

John's Visions

Christ and golden lampstands—*Revelation 1:10-20*
Open door—*Revelation 4:1*
Rainbow and throne—*Revelation 4:2-3*
Twenty-four elders—*Revelation 4:4*
Seven lamps—*Revelation 4:5*
Sea of glass—*Revelation 4:6*
Four living creatures—*Revelation 4:6-8*
Book with seven seals—*Revelation 5:1-5*
Golden bowls—*Revelation 5:8*
Six seals—*Revelation 6*
Four horses—*Revelation 6:2-8*
Earthquake and celestial phenomena—*Revelation 6:12-14*
Four angels—*Revelation 7:1*
Sealing of the 144,000—*Revelation 7:2-8*
Seventh seal and seven angels—*Revelation 8–11*
Censer—*Revelation 8:5*
Hail and fire—*Revelation 8:7*
Mountain cast into sea—*Revelation 8:8-9*
Falling star—*Revelation 8:10-11; 9:1*
Third of sun, moon, stars darkened—*Revelation 8:12*
Bottomless pit—*Revelation 9:2*
Locusts—*Revelation 9:3-11*
Four angels loosed from Euphrates—*Revelation 9:14*
Army of horsemen—*Revelation 9:16-19*
Angel having a book—*Revelation 10:1-10*
Seven thunders—*Revelation 10:3-4*
Measurement of temple—*Revelation 11:1-2*
Two witnesses—*Revelation 11:3-12*
Court of Gentiles—*Revelation 11:2*
Two olive trees, two lampstands—*Revelation 11:4*
Beast out of bottomless pit—*Revelation 11:7*
Fall of city—*Revelation 11:13*

Second and third woes—*Revelation 11:14*
Birth of male child—*Revelation 12*
Red dragon—*Revelation 12:3-17*
War in heaven—*Revelation 12:7-9*
Beast rising out of sea—*Revelation 13:1-10*
Beast coming out of earth—*Revelation 13:11-18*
Lamb on Mount Zion—*Revelation 14:1-5*
Angel and everlasting gospel—*Revelation 14:6-7*
Angel proclaims fall of Babylon—*Revelation 14:8-13*
Son of Man with sickle—*Revelation 14:15-16*
Angel reaping harvest—*Revelation 14:14-20*
Angel coming out of temple—*Revelation 14:17-19*
Angel with power over fire—*Revelation 14:18*
Vine and winepress—*Revelation 14:18-20*
Angels with seven last plagues—*Revelation 15*
Sea of glass—*Revelation 15:2*
Temple opened—*Revelation 15:5*
Plague upon men with mark of beast—*Revelation 16:2*
Sea turned to blood—*Revelation 16:3*
Seven angels, seven bowls of God's wrath—*Revelation 16; 17*
Destruction of Babylon—*Revelation 18*
Multitude praising God—*Revelation 19:1-9*
Jesus' second coming—*Revelation 19:11-16*
Angel in sun—*Revelation 19:17-21*
Satan bound 1000 years—*Revelation 20:1-3*
Thrones of judgment, resurrection, Satan loosed—*Revelation 20:1-10*
Great White Throne—*Revelation 20:11*
Book of life opened—*Revelation 20:12*
Death and hell—*Revelation 20:14*
New Jerusalem—*Revelation 21*
River of life—*Revelation 22:1*
Tree of life—*Revelation 22:2*

VOICE OF THE ARCHANGEL

Archangel shouts at rapture—*1 Thessalonians 4:16-17*

Voice of angels—*2 Thessalonians 1:7*

Angels heavily involved in end-time events—*Revelation 5:11; 7:1-2,11; 8:2,4,6,13; 9:14-15; 10:10; 12:7,9; 14:10; 15:1,6-8; 16:1; 17:1; 21:9,12*

See Angels

WAR OF ARMAGEDDON

Prior to second coming—*Revelation 16:16*

Catastrophic series of battles—*Daniel 11:40-45; Joel 3:9-17; Zechariah 14:1-3; Revelation 16:14-16*

Devastating to humanity—*Matthew 24:22*

Place of final battle—*Revelation 16:14,16*

Antichrist's allies assembled—*Psalm 2:1-6; Joel 3:9-11; Revelation 16:12-16*

Antichrist's armies at Bozrah—*Jeremiah 49:13-14*

Horrific battle from Bozrah to Valley of Jehoshaphat—*Jeremiah 49:20-22; Joel 3:12-13; Zechariah 14:12-15*

Antichrist's campaign into Egypt—*Daniel 11:40-45*

Babylon destroyed—*Isaiah 13–14; Jeremiah 50–51; Zechariah 5:5-11; Revelation 17–18*

Ascent on Mount of Olives—*Joel 3:14-17; Zechariah 14:3-5; Matthew 24:29-31; Revelation 16:17-21; 19:11-21*

Siege of Jerusalem—*Zechariah 14:2*

Jerusalem falls—*Micah 4:11–5:1; Zechariah 12–14*

War on great day of God—*Revelation 16:14*

Israel experiences regeneration—*Psalm 79:1-13; Isaiah 64:1-12; Hosea 6:1-11; Joel 2:28-32; Zechariah 12:10; Romans 11:25-27*

Second coming ends it—*Isaiah 34:1-7; Micah 2:12-13; Habakkuk 3:3; Revelation 19:11-21*

No one would survive if not for Christ coming—*Matthew 24:22*

WARNINGS TO THE WICKED

Every eye will see—*Revelation 1:7*

Retribution—*2 Thessalonians 1:8*

Shame—*Mark 8:38*

Will be mourning—*Matthew 24:30*

See Second Coming

WATCHFULNESS

Be on alert—*Acts 20:31; 1 Corinthians 16:13*
Blessedness of—*Luke 12:37; Revelation 16:15*
Christ our example—*Matthew 26:38,40; Luke 6:12*
Commanded—*Mark 13:37; 1 Thessalonians 5:6; 1 Peter 4:7; Revelation 3:2*
Danger of neglecting—*Matthew 24:48-51; 25:5,8,12; Revelation 3:3*
Devote yourselves to prayer—*Colossians 4:2*
In all things—*2 Timothy 4:5*
In view of Christ's return—*Matthew 24:42; 25:13; Mark 13:35-36*
In view of incessant assaults of devil—*1 Peter 5:8*
In view of liability to temptation—*Matthew 26:41*
Pray—*Luke 21:36; Ephesians 6:18*
Watch and pray—*Matthew 26:41*
With sobriety—*1 Thessalonians 5:6; 1 Peter 4:7*
With steadfastness in faith—*1 Corinthians 16:13*
See Eternal Perspective

WEAPONS (EZEKIEL INVASION)

Buckler, shield, swords—*Ezekiel 38:4*
Shield and helmet—*Ezekiel 38:5*
Israel burns weapons—*Ezekiel 39:9*
See Ezekiel Invasion

WITCHCRAFT

Do not consult mediums, psychics—*Leviticus 19:31*
God opposes those who consult mediums—*Leviticus 20:6*
Medium at Endor—*1 Samuel 28:7-9*
Mediums, psychics, sorceresses to be executed in Old Testament law—*Exodus 22:18; Leviticus 20:27*
Saul banned mediums and psychics—*1 Samuel 28:3*
See Occultism

WOES

First woe: Fifth trumpet judgment—*Revelation 9:1-12*
Second woe: Sixth trumpet judgment—*Revelation 9:13-21*
Third woe: Seventh trumpet judgment—*Revelation 11:15-19*
See Trumpet Judgments

WOMAN OF REVELATION 12

Israel as the wife of God—*Isaiah 54:5-6; Jeremiah 3:6-8; 31:32; Ezekiel 16:32; Hosea 2:16*

Imagery of sun, moon, and 12 stars points to Israel—*1 Chronicles 23:31; 2 Chronicles 2:4; 8:13*

Dragon standing before woman giving birth (to Christ) is Satan—*Revelation 12:4 (compare with Herod's murder of male children—Matthew 2:13-18; Luke 4:28-29)*

Child caught up to heaven—*Revelation 12:5; see also Acts 1:9; 2:33; Hebrews 1:1-3; 12:2*

Woman (Jews) flee into wilderness—*Revelation 12:5-6*

WORD OF GOD (BIBLE)

Bereans tested Paul's teaching from Scripture—*Acts 17:11*
Blessed are those who hear and obey—*Luke 11:28*
Correctly explain Word—*2 Timothy 2:15*
Do not add to, subtract—*Deuteronomy 4:2; 12:32; Revelation 22:18-19*
Do not distort Word of God—*2 Corinthians 4:2*
God's Word flawless—*Proverbs 30:5-6*
God's Word is truth—*John 17:17*
God's Word is wonderful—*Psalm 119:129-130*
Jesus' words never pass away—*Matthew 24:35*
Learn Scriptures from childhood—*2 Timothy 3:15*
Let word of Christ dwell in you—*Colossians 3:16*
Love God's Word—*Psalm 119:97-106*
Man depends on God's Word—*Matthew 4:4*
Scriptures point to Jesus—*John 5:39*

Sword of Spirit—*Ephesians 6:17*
Word inspired by Holy Spirit—*2 Peter 1:21*
Word keeps us from sinning—*Psalm 119:9-16*
Word of God is living—*Hebrews 4:12-13*
See Scripture

WORD OF GOD (JESUS)

In the beginning—*John 1:1*
At second coming—*Revelation 19:13*

WORLD RELIGION (RELIGIOUS BABYLON)

Description of—*Revelation 17:1-7*
Interpretation of—*Revelation 17:8-18*
Controls nations—*Revelation 17:9*
Outwardly glorious, inwardly corrupt—*Revelation 17:4*
Persecutes true believers—*Revelation 17:6*
Powerful political clout—*Revelation 17:12-13*
Unfaithful to truth—*Revelation 17:1,5,15-16*
Worldwide in impact—*Revelation 17:15*
Worship of Antichrist—*1 Timothy 4:1-4; 2 Timothy 3:1-5; 4:1-4; 2 Peter 2:1; 1 John 2:18-19; Jude 4; Revelation 17:1-6*
Violently overthrown—*Revelation 17:16*

WORLD RULER

Beast—*Revelation 13:1-10*
Counterfeit signs and wonders—*2 Thessalonians 2:9-10*
Destiny is lake of fire—*Revelation 19:20*
Dominion during tribulation—*Revelation 13*
False prophet promotes worship of him—*Revelation 13:11-12*
Headquarters in Rome—*Revelation 17:8-9; compare with Daniel 2; 7*
Is coming—*1 John 2:18*
Makes covenant with Israel—*Daniel 9:27*
Man of lawlessness—*2 Thessalonians 2:1-10*

Rises out of "sea" (Gentile nations)—*Revelation 13:1; 17:15*

Seeks his own kingdom—*Revelation 13*

Speaks arrogant words—*2 Thessalonians 2:4*

Will eventually rule whole world—*Revelation 13:7*

Will be destroyed by Jesus at second coming—*Revelation 19:11-16*

See Antichrist

WORMWOOD

Star ("great mountain") from heaven that poisons waters of earth—*Revelation 8:10-11*

Burning with fire—*Revelation 8:10*

Many human beings die—*Revelation 8:11*

WORRY

Antidote to worry—*Philippians 4:6-7*

Anxious heart weighs us down—*Proverbs 12:25*

Banish anxiety from heart—*Ecclesiastes 11:10*

Cast anxiety on God—*1 Peter 5:7*

Circumstances need not cause worry—*Luke 8:22-25*

Do not be anxious—*Philippians 4:6*

God consoles us—*Psalm 94:19*

Jesus' advice on anxiety—*Matthew 6:25-34*

Life's worries—*Mark 4:19*

Nonproductive—*Matthew 6:27-28*

The Lord always at hand—*Acts 2:25-28*

Worry blinds eyes to truth—*Matthew 13:22*

See Eternal Perspective; Watchfulness

WORSHIP IN HEAVEN DURING TRIBULATION

Twenty-four elders and four living creatures worship God—*Revelation 19:4*

144,000 sing a new song—*Revelation 14:3-5*

God's temple in heaven—*Revelation 11:19*

Jesus and Father receive same worship—*Revelation 4–5*
Others join in the praise—*Revelation 19:5-6*
Saints worship and praise God—*Revelation 15:1-8*

WRATH OF GOD

Imminent—*Ephesians 5:6; Colossians 3:6*
Church not appointed to—*1 Thessalonians 1:10; 5:9*
Poured out like fire—*Nahum 1:6; see also Deuteronomy 4:24; Jeremiah 4:4; Malachi 3:2*
Entire tribulation characterized by wrath—*Zephaniah 1:15,18; 1 Thessalonians 1:10; Revelation 6:17; 14:7,10; 19:2*
Receiving mark of beast invites God's wrath—*Revelation 14:10; see also Psalm 75:8; Isaiah 51:17; Jeremiah 25:15-16*
Present reality—*Romans 1:18; 1 Thessalonians 2:16*

Effects of God's Wrath

Affliction—*Psalm 88:7*
Drought—*Deuteronomy 11:17*
Leprosy—*Numbers 12:10*
Pestilence—*Ezekiel 14:19*
Plagues—*2 Samuel 24:10-25*
Slaughter—*Ezekiel 9:8*
Destruction—*Ezekiel 5:15*
Defeat—*2 Chronicles 28:9*
Exile—*2 Kings 23:26-27; Ezekiel 19:12-13*
See Judgment

WRATH OF THE LAMB

Wrath of Lamb—*Revelation 6:15-16; see also Revelation 6:1,3,5,7,9,12; 8:1*

ZECHARIAH, BOOK OF

Demonstrated importance of building the temple—*Zechariah 1–8*

Christ betrayed for 30 pieces of silver—*Zechariah 11:12-13*

Christ pierced on cross—*Zechariah 12:10*

Israel to mourn and plead for the Messiah—*Zechariah 12:10*

Armageddon—*Zechariah 14:1-5*

Christ will come again in glory—*Zechariah 14:4*

Cosmic disturbances at the second coming—*Zechariah 14:6; see also Acts 2:19-20*

God will live among His people during millennial kingdom—*Zechariah 14:16-19*

ZEPHANIAH, BOOK OF

Judgment imminent—*Zephaniah 1:2-3; 2:2; 3:6-7*

Day of the Lord approaching—*Zephaniah 1:7,14-16; 3:8*

Horror of Armageddon—*Zephaniah 3:8; see also Revelation 16:14*

Millennial kingdom—*Zephaniah 3:9-20*

Pure worship in millennial kingdom—*Zephaniah 3:9*

Jewish nation regathered and purified—*Zephaniah 3:10-13*

Divine Messiah will reign—*Zephaniah 3:15*

Security for all—*Zephaniah 3:16*

Israel restored to land—*Zephaniah 3:20*

Other Great Harvest House Books
by Ron Rhodes

BOOKS ABOUT THE BIBLE
Commonly Misunderstood Bible Verses
The Book of Bible Promises
Find It Fast in the Bible
The Complete Guide to Bible Translations
What Does the Bible Say About...?

BOOKS ABOUT OTHER IMPORTANT TOPICS
5-Minute Apologetics for Today
Angels Among Us
The Complete Guide to Christian Denominations
Conviction Without Compromise
Northern Storm Rising
The Popular Dictionary of Bible Prophecy
The Truth Behind Ghosts, Mediums, and Psychic Phenomena
The Wonder of Heaven
The 10 Most Important Things You Can Say to a Catholic
The 10 Most Important Things You Can Say to a Jehovah's Witness
The 10 Most Important Things You Can Say to a Mormon
The 10 Things You Need to Know About Islam
Reasoning from the Scriptures with Catholics
Reasoning from the Scriptures with the Mormons
Reasoning from the Scriptures with Muslims

QUICK REFERENCE GUIDES
Archaeology and the Bible: What You Need to Know
The Middle East Conflict: What You Need to Know
Halloween: What You Need to Know
Christian Views of War: What You Need to Know
Homosexuality: What You Need to Know
World Religions: What You Need to Know
Islam: What You Need to Know
Jehovah's Witnesses: What You Need to Know